T0195678

THE LAST OF THE BLACK HAWKS: MEMOIRS OF CHILDHOOD FRIENDS

THOMAS CALHOUN MD,
WILBUR H. JENKINS JR. JD

authorHOUSE®

AuthorHouse™
1663 Liberty Drive
Bloomington, IN 47403
www.authorhouse.com
Phone: 833-262-8899

Published by AuthorHouse 03/24/2022

ISBN: 978-1-6655-3457-4 (sc)
ISBN: 978-1-6655-3455-0 (hc)
ISBN: 978-1-6655-3456-7 (e)

Library of Congress Control Number: 2021916204

Print information available on the last page.

Any people depicted in stock imagery provided by Getty Images are models, and such images are being used for illustrative purposes only.
Certain stock imagery © Getty Images.

This book is printed on acid-free paper.

CONTENTS

To our wives, Shirley and Doris; our children, Tom Jr., Christine, Kathy, Maria, Kimberly, and Wilbur "Butch"; our grandchildren; and Furman Adams, the other Black Hawk still alive.

ACKNOWLEDGEMENTS

My sincere thanks to our oldest daughter, Christine, who tirelessly and patiently formatted the book, to Kimberly, Jenks daughter, who having published two books herself, reviewed and offered many corrections, and Roz Campbell, who did the original typing, and finally, my brother, Bill, who helped me recall many of our childhood experiences.

True Friendship[1]

A faithful friend is a sturdy shelter; he who finds one finds a treasure. A faithful friendship is beyond price, no sum can balance his worth. A faithful friend is a life-saving remedy, such as he who fears God finds; for he who fears God behaves accordingly and his friend will be like himself.

---

[1] Sirach 7, 14–17: The New American Bible, 1989–1990 Edition, 704.

INTRODUCTION

This is a collection of memories of a group of young Black males, growing up in the segregated south, in Jacksonville, Florida, in the late 1940s and a legendary basketball team called the *Black Hawks*, which bonded them together.

The Authors—Dr. Thomas Calhoun (me) and Wilbur (Jenk) Jenkins, JD—were best friends for over seventy years. Jenk died on July 7, 2020, unable to see the publication of the book, which is dedicated to him and those noted in the dedication.

The members of the *Black Hawks*, in addition to me and Jenk, were Dr. Earl Thomas Cullins (now deceased), Reverend Henry (Diddy) Rhim (now deceased), Furman Adams, and Paschal Collins, whom the authors could not locate. Oscar Fletcher and Dr. Alvin White were also members and are both deceased.

Much of the excitement of the memoirs involved Jenk and me and our experiences on the American Tennis Association (ATA) circuit.

Were my experiences with health problems and death seen at an early age, signs of predestation, and were all of those accidents—near misses if you would—coordinated by my guardian angel or just acts of serendipity in the scheme of life?

Who would have thought that our introduction to tennis by two pretty girls would presage a lifelong pursuit that we enjoyed and participated in well into our eighties?

The racism, the bombing, and some of the other events described may seem like the subject of a cheap soap opera, but often truth is stranger than fiction.

Dr. Earl Thomas Cullins was the first Black surgeon given operating privileges in Jacksonville, where he lived and died. He was also a member of the Alpha Phi Alpha fraternity and collaborated with Drs. McIntosch, Richard Hunter, and Dawkins to found and build the Northwest Jacksonville Medical Complex, one of the first African-American multispecialty medical groups in Jacksonville, Florida.

He was born on September 12, 1932, in Jacksonville and passed on May 29, 2007, from complications of Parkinson's Disease.[2]

Jenk became an Attorney, and after graduating from Howard University, he worked with the Equal Employment Opportunity Commission (EEOC) in DC, along with Attorney Clarence Thomas. Jenk would become an avid civil rights advocate.

Some years later, Attorney Clarence Thomas would become a Supreme Court Justice.

The poem Jenk wrote for Arthur Ashe, with whom he became good friends, displays a depth of his character I had not seen before.

Jenk was one of the first Black males invited to play tennis at the segregated US Open Tennis Championships in 1957 in New York City.

On September 9, 1968, Arthur Ashe Jr. would become the first and only Black male to date to win the US Open Tennis men's singles championship at the West Side Tennis Club in Forest Hills, New York.

Jenk, his family, and my family are shown in a number of photographs, as are a number of tennis events in our lives. Furman also relates some highlights from his life.

I was privileged to become the second Black president of the Medical Dental Staff of Providence Hospital in DC and performed the first minimally invasive surgical procedure, a laparoscopic cholecystectomy (removal of a diseased gall bladder) at the hospital, which had previously denied me admitting and operating privileges.

Several years earlier, I had been asked to be the President of the Medical Dental Staff, but I declined. In my mind, the time was not right.

The Black Hawks are evidence of the strength and resiliency of a group of African American males, undaunted by the challenges of growing up in a segregated south during and just after the Great Depression.

---

[2] https://www.legacy.com>obituaries>name-earl-cull.

CHAPTER 1

THE EARLY YEARS

In 1936, I would have been four years old. I remember running after my mother, Sylvia Barnes (Syl), and asking her not to leave. She and Walter Thompson, as I understood at that young age, were going off to be married, and I did not want her to leave. My reward for accepting their leaving was a five-cent box of chocolate snap cookies, a favorite at that time.

I was staying at 1100 West State Street in Jacksonville, Florida, with Tom and Luella Calhoun, Sylvia's aunt and uncle. I was told I was named after Tom Calhoun, whom everyone called Bud. My name on the birth certificate is Tom Calhoun, and my biological father was J. C. Borders. He was twenty-two. I never met J. C. Borders.

On one occasion, as an adult, I asked Syl about him, and she said he was just a friend. I sensed she was embarrassed about discussing it, so I did not pursue the matter further.

Our house was a wood duplex with a tin roof. Even now, I can recall the sound of raindrops on the roof. At times, it was comforting, and at other times, it was a perceived threat, especially with stormy weather.

Numbers 1110 and 1112 were the only two houses on that side of the block.

Our house had four rooms. The front room was the living room, and it had a fireplace on the north side. There were two windows, one on the east side facing State Street and the other on the south side facing the driveway. The second and third rooms were the bedrooms, each with windows facing the driveway.

I say "driveway" even though we never had a car; however, whenever people who had a car would visit, they would often park in the driveway.

Years later, when I did get a car, that driveway allowed me to park off the street when I returned home for a visit.

In the front room, there was a sofa and a radio with a small table and an oil lamp. There was no electricity, so we used oil lamps. The battery-powered radio was on a small table near the south window, and I would often listen to *The Lone Ranger* and *The Shadow*, two of my favorite shows.

I enjoyed all kinds of music, and it seems like I was singing all the time, memorizing songs that were popular at that time.

At Christmastime, I washed those two windows in the front room on the inside and the outside. I took much pride in hanging a red-and-green Christmas wreath on each window.

I don't recall having a lot of toys over the years, but I do remember getting a cap pistol, a pair of roller skates, and, when I was about nine or ten, a bicycle. Around that time, I began delivering the *Jacksonville Journal*, the evening newspaper.

This was about the time Jenk and I became friends. Over the years, Wilbur H. Jenkins Jr. and I would become best friends, and much of our history and activities together will be forthcoming later in the book.

As I was growing up, my room was the second room from the front, and Bud and Luella slept in the third room. The fourth room was the kitchen with the wood-burning stove. A window opened onto the south side, and there was a door leading out to an open porch. At some point, this was closed in and became a fifth room. The bathroom was located here. It was also where we stored my bike and other items, with a door that opened out to the backyard.

In the backyard, which was fenced off, we grew a few stalks of corn and sugarcane in season. We also had a few hens and a mean rooster that would often attack me when I went to get the eggs the hens had laid.

I finally chopped that rooster's head off, and we had him for dinner! I hope that does not sound gross, but that was the reality of the times, and of course, Momma had told me to do it.

Luella, whom I called "Momma," would cook some delicious meals. We had very meager meals, but I don't ever remember being hungry. For breakfast, we had regular meals of grits, eggs, bacon, and hot biscuits.

Dinner often consisted of meatloaf, liver and onions, fried or smothered chicken, pork chops, collard greens, snap beans, tomatoes, and cornbread or hot buttered biscuits.

At some point, the Wonder Bread company opened on Kings Road, several blocks from our house, and we could buy a loaf of bread for a nickel. A dozen white sugarcoated doughnuts cost twenty-five cents. In the early evenings, we could often smell the aromas of the bread being baked, wafting in the summer breeze past our house, a really special treat. The loaf of bread was unsliced at that time, which meant we could cut our slices as we chose. Momma was always rather strict with the bread slices because we did not want to throw food away.

We did have a small "ice box," which allowed for twenty-five pounds of ice. In Jacksonville, Florida, the temperature was often in the mid- to high nineties.

Dessert would sometimes be lemon meringue, coconut pie, chocolate cake, sweet potato pies, or a dish called "sweet potato pone," made with sweet potatoes, sugar, nutmeg, and cinnamon. (Man, I wish I had saved that recipe!)

On some Saturdays and Sundays during the summer months, we made homemade ice cream. This was great fun for me because as I churned the ice cream maker, I would have to taste frequent samples to see if it was ready.

I remember Bud was present on many of these occasions, and he and Momma seemed very happy.

Living next door in 1112 was the Williams family. There was Mr. Williams; his wife, Clara; and their children, Calvin, James (Jamie), Erma Mae (the oldest), Mozell, and Bernice, who was the youngest. I can't recall how she looked, but I was told that Bernice grew into a very beautiful young lady.

Jamie is still my friend today, and we are in contact two or three times a month by exchanging emails and phone calls.

For a time, I went to A. L. Lewis Public School and occasionally the Methodist Church School that was located one block to the east on Kings Road (Highway 1, now 95). It is still called that today. I remember crying and protesting about having to go to school there on a particular day but that afternoon, after school, I told Momma, "I had so much fun today."

I believe all of my schooling from about third grade until completion of the tenth grade was at St. Pius Catholic School. As I recall, I would often get into fights at A. L. Lewis School, so Momma decided to send me to the Catholic school.

I am not sure if the tuition was a dollar a week or a dollar a month. Sometimes we didn't have the money to pay, but the nuns let me stay. St. Pius was three long blocks in a straight line from our house on State Street, so I could and did easily walk to and from school. It was the only Catholic school that Coloreds could attend in Jacksonville, Florida, at that time.

I believe I immediately and eagerly accepted the change. Classes were taught by the strict, White Nuns, from the Order of Sisters of St. Joseph and two White Jesuit Priests. The school was bordered by Davis Street on the South on which the Ritz Movie Theater was located and State Street on the east side. Saturdays were the best days to go to the movies because you could watch Red Ryder and other cowboy movies for only twenty-five cents. The Priests lived in the rectory on the west boundary, Johnson Street, and the front of the school was on Lee Street, the north boundary.

In the beginning, I remember I still got into fights. I do not know why, but when this would happen, one of the Priests would have us put on boxing gloves and "duke it out" for a few minutes. No one was ever injured, and eventually the fights stopped. I remember one fight I had with Allen. I hit him with a closed fist to the jaw, and he fell to the ground. After this, word got around not to mess with Tommy!

I really enjoyed school and all the classes. I learned mathematics by memorizing addition, subtraction, and multiplication using the black-and-white tablet that was standard at that time with those tables on the back cover.

I enjoyed reading and read all the books I could. One of my favorite series was by Edgar Rice Burroughs, the author of stories about Tarzan. I had to have my homework completed before dark because we had oil lamps and a heater that used oil, and we had to be careful about spending too much money for oil during the winter months.

I don't believe the temperature got below freezing in Jacksonville, but temperatures in the fifties and forties were cold!

School started every morning at Saint Pius with prayer. As I recall, most of us were not Catholics at that time. The school had a Basement that we used during inclement weather for parties and school plays and also as the lunch hall.

On the first floor was the Church. I soon became very interested in becoming a Catholic, but Momma wouldn't allow it at that time. On Sundays, Momma and I would go to the Baptist church, which was around the corner to the north, on Dewitt Street.

Wilbur H. Jenkins Jr. (Jenk) and Earl Thomas Cullins lived on Dewitt Street. I always enjoyed going to their houses because they had electricity and inside toilets, and when the weather was bad and we could not play ball outside, we played checkers or bid whist.

Every Sunday, we could hear the choir singing from our back porch. There was also an evening service for the Baptist Young Peoples' Union (BYPU).

I did not like spending all that time in Church—an hour or so for morning worship and again for the BYPU service in the afternoon. Over time, I became more indoctrinated into Catholicism, and finally, I was allowed to be baptized and became a Catholic. Ultimately, I became an altar boy, which allowed me to serve at all the Masses. At that time, most of the Mass was in Latin, and I quickly memorized the Confiteor and several other common prayers in Latin used at Mass, so it is not surprising to me that at that time, I wanted to become a Priest. Moreover, it was during these years that my Catholic faith was shaped. It would become and remain an active part of my life up to the present time.

I had never seen a Colored Priest or Colored Nun, and it would be some twenty years later, after my sophomore year in medical school at Meharry Medical College in Nashville, Tennessee, before I saw Bishop Harold Perry, a Negro Priest, in Mound Bayou, Mississippi, while I was working as an Extern. There will be much more discussion about this later.

The houses at 1110 and 1112 West State Street faced east. There were two large sycamore trees in front of the house, one with its roots coming under our house and the other off to the right of the house. This was the tree where we local boys threw ropes around the lower hanging limbs to make our swings. The tree directly in front of 1110, our house, afforded us a challenging task for climbing to get on top of the house.

One of the decisions we had to make to transition, in our minds, to big boys from around seven or eight to ten years old was to jump off the roof of 1112. Looking back, I realize the height was fifteen to twenty feet, but no one was ever injured following our many jumps to the open dirt field. I can recall one significant jump from another facility during this time. As noted earlier, St. Pius Catholic School had a basement. To reach the basement from the outside meant going down about eight to ten steps. A tin roof covered the steps with a supporting bar, four to five feet across, attached to a vertical support beam. The crossbar was no more than six feet from the ground, so with little effort, most of us boys could leap up and grab the bar for chin-ups or to swing on. One of the feats that defined the boy's "manhood" in our minds, if you would, was to swing from the bar to the basement floor, avoiding the last step.

After I had jumped, Carl T. was unlucky on that particular day because at the end of his attempt, his foot (don't remember which foot) hit the last step in a funny manner, as I understood at that time, and he twisted his ankle. I can recall very clearly now, eighty-plus years later his screaming in pain and the foot looking "funny." I am thinking I was eleven or twelve years old, but I immediately grabbed his foot with both hands and "relocated" the ankle. I could see the foot return to its proper position, and I could hear and feel the "relocation" process. Carl was instantly better, and we continued playing. It was lunch time, and he was not in any pain as I remember.

I do not know what made me do what I did, and I never thought any more about it until I began writing these memoirs.

When one of the Nuns came to check on us, no doubt after hearing Carl scream in pain, a girl standing nearby told her that "he (me) pushed him." I never understood why she said that, but Carl and I immediately told the nun that was not true. I do not know who she was, and I cannot recall ever having any connection with her, either before or after the event. In hindsight, this may have been one of those early experiences that sharpened my desire to become a doctor and later a Surgeon, though I am sure I had no such thoughts at that time.

Three other incidents come to mind relating to health. Across the street from 1110 at the corner of State and Cleveland Streets was "Doc's" neighborhood store. Doc was the White owner. I cannot recall ever knowing his name. It was one of many neighborhood stores that sold different food, drinks, and medical products such as cough syrup and pain medicines. Over some period of time, I worked at Doc's, starting with cleaning the floors, taking out the trash, and helping restock supplies. At some point, I had earned the position that I could sell products to customers and ring up at the cash register, a sign of his trust in me.

On one sunny day, while I was sitting on our front porch, I saw a White male walking out of Doc's and falling face down to the ground. I would find out later that he had died, apparently from a heart attack. Age-wise, I was about eleven or twelve, but somehow, I knew he had died.

The second incident occurred sometime later. I remember as I was leaving the house to begin my morning paper route. (At this time, I had an evening paper route also since school was out for the summer.) There was a Colored man lying face down on the ground in the back yard of the house on the corner of State and Cleveland Street across from "Doc's" and South of our house. I remember telling Momma this before I left, but I cannot remember what happened, as I went on to start delivering the papers.

When I returned home after delivering my papers, the body was gone. I don't believe we ever found out what happened. The third incident was similar. Again sometime later, as I was leaving for my morning paper route, while rounding the corner on State and Dewitt Streets, which was on the block north of Doc's and our house, I saw another Colored man lying face down, apparently dead. I never found out any information about any of these incidents. I went back and told Momma about this also before leaving for my paper deliveries.

There was another defining event, in my mind, which pretty much completed my desire to become a Doctor.

Leading up to the front porch of our house were five steps. There was a swing and a "rocking chair" on the front porch but no rails on any side. On this particular day, Momma was sitting in her rocking chair, and I was playing on the porch. On three separate occasions, while I was playing near the edge of the porch, I fell on those roots from the sycamore tree.

Momma told me to stop playing before I hurt myself. I was not hurt, and like many nine-year olds1 at that age, I did not stop playing. I fell a second time, and again, I was not injured. Again she told me to stop playing, and of course, I continued playing. I fell a third time, having not adhered to what Momma had told me. This time, I was hurt pretty bad because I recall lying in bed and having a lot of pain. I do not know the timeframe, but I can remember looking up and seeing this dark-skinned man, a doctor, whom I would find out later was Dr. I. E. Williams (long ago deceased). As he was walking in from the front porch, it seemed that I ached with every step I heard, but as soon as I looked up and saw him, all my pain stopped. I do not know what medicines he prescribed, but I do know that then and there, I decided that when I grew up, I would become a doctor so that I could help people feel better.

My next contact with Dr. Williams occurred sometime later and involved my brother Bill (William Manuel Thompson) born September 25, 1937. He has given me permission to use his name.

He remembers this differently from me, but I am sure of this event. As we were growing up, our circle of friends and playmates were different, mainly because of our age difference. I am five years older. On the grounds of St. Pius, there was a basketball court, and often after school hours, the boys would pick up a game. It happened that in the late afternoon one day, I had returned to St. Pius—for what reason, I cannot recall—just in time as it were to find out that Bill had broken his leg just below the knee. He was in a lot of pain. He would have been seven or eight years old, and I was in my early teens. I picked him up and carried him about a block and a half to Dr. Williams's office, which was near the Ritz Theater. I remember walking with Bill in my arms, crying and begging Dr. Williams to help my brother. I said something to the effect that I would find work to pay him as soon as I could. I can't recall the details, but I know Bill was taken to Brewster's Hospital, which was the hospital for Colored people.

The George A. Brewster Hospital and School of Nurse Training was the first Black Hospital in Jacksonville and served African Americans from 1901 until 1966 when it was demolished. During this time, Negroes could not be admitted to White hospitals, nor were there any Negro Doctors or Nurses; they were employed as Cooks and cleaning personnel.

A plaster cast was applied, and the leg would heal over time but with a very crooked angle, resulting in a significant limp. As this was during the time of rapid growth, the limp became more exaggerated.

Bill recalls that he was playing football some years later and was clipped from behind, breaking the leg. He had surgery and was in a long hip plaster cast and bedridden for several months. This was much later because I recall visiting him as an adult with Carrie, a lady friend of mine.

This was during the time he was considering become a Priest. Reflecting on my earlier years, several personal health risks come to mind. The first may have been when I was seven or eight years old. I was running from Doc's store across the street after having bought something, and as I was about to cross the street there seems to have been an invisible hand that abruptly stopped me. Had I continued running, I would have been hit by an oncoming car with who knows what results?

Another important event occurred during this period. I was working on the wood truck of one of the owners in the neighborhood, and after we had delivered some wood to a customer, I was playing on the "running board" and slipped and fell. The truck, not a very big one as I recall, ran over my left leg, but I got up and back on the truck immediately, uninjured. I do not believe anyone ever knew because I did not say anything about it.

There was another occasion when I was staying on West Beaver Street with Syl, and I stepped on a "rusty nail," which punctured my knee—I'm not sure which one. Rusty nails, we knew, were bad news because they could cause "blood poison" as I understood at that time. I remember getting "spider's web" and putting that on the area, which was a common treatment for cuts, I thought, and I was soon healed.

Another rather frightful event occurred during that growth period, as I will call it.

Often when I was running or jumping, I would suck my tongue. I was playing in the back yard at Momma's house and had just thrown an imaginary spear when I bit my tongue! Blood started gushing out, and I ran into the house and told Momma. She gave me some warm salt water to rinse my mouth, and as best as I can remember, I was "all healed" in a few days.

The Early Years—Later

I rarely had to be seen by a Doctor. The first and only time growing up, as I noted, was when I fell off the front porch. The other happened one evening when I was going to St. Pius School because I was going to be promoted to an Eagle Scout. I would have just turned thirteen or fourteen years old, the age I believe one had to be in order to become an Eagle Scout in 1945.

As I was leaving the house, I became very "short of breath."

I came back in the house, and I remember Momma contacting Dr. Williams.

In retrospect, I believe I had some variant of rheumatic fever, which was common among young children at the time. As I had noted earlier, I began attending St. Pius Catholic School because Momma did not want me to get in fights, which I did almost daily while attending school at A. L. Lewis.

A.L. Lewis School was the only public Elementary School for Negroes in Jacksonville at that time. Abraham L. Lewis was the first Black millionaire in the state of Florida. He had made his money via the insurance industry and also constructed the Lincoln Golf and Country Club in Jacksonville, which will be noted later. History indicates that although he was a millionaire, he was still subjected to the strict Jim Crow laws in force at the time.

I did not know why or how Momma decided on St. Pius because none of us were Catholic at that time. In fact, as I recall, no one in our immediate household was of any religious denomination.

I don't remember Bud (Uncle Tom Calhoun, after whom I was named) ever going to any Church. There were four churches in the neighborhood. Second Baptist Church on Kings Road was one, and Momma and I went there on some Sundays, including Easter. The other, Shiloh, was located at Kings Road (Highway 1) one street over and about three blocks from our house. As I recall, I went several times on my own. I did not like it because the services were too long. As I noted earlier, there was an evening service called "BYPU" (Baptist Young People's Union), and I would have to go back for that. There was a Methodist Church one block away from the back of the house on Dewitt Street, where Jenk and Earl lived. On Sunday mornings, we could hear singing coming from the Church. The fourth was Saint Pius Catholic Church (spcc).

According to a Google search, St. Pius Catholic Church was the "Mother Church of African American Catholics in Jacksonville, Florida." The mission statement is "to know, love and serve God and share and build upon our rich Catholic African American Culture. We proclaim Jesus as Lord through worship and service, education and social ministries." (spcc) http://stpiusjax.org.

Originally, in Jacksonville, Negro Catholics were a part of the Immaculate Conception Parish, the White church. At that time, seating for "Coloreds or Negroes, alternate names" was restricted to side benches, and there were no Colored altar boys, nor were any Negroes allowed to sing in the choirs.

On September 14, 1919, the first Mass for the Negroes was celebrated in the schoolhouse behind Immaculate Conception Church. It was attended by seventeen individuals, who gave a collection of $7.70. Earlier in 1919, a site had been purchased by Bishop Curley for $12,000, half a city block away at West State and Lee Streets. The funds were for the construction of a church and school for the Coloreds. It was dedicated on February 27, 1921, and cost $55,000. Money was donated by the Josephite Fathers, with substantial contributions from Bishop Curley and John E. Banks, DD, Director of the Catholic Board for Missionary work among Colored people. (The preceding dollar information was obtained via Google search.)

I would have been eight years old when I started St. Pius in 1940. I believe the cost was a dollar a week. There were weeks when we did not have the tuition, but I was allowed to stay. At that time, Momma was not working out of the house. She would take in clothes for washing and ironing for some of the neighbors. For a time, she sold "moonshine" for twenty-five cents a shot. We were very happy when she had some fifty-cent sales.

This was during the time of Prohibition, and selling whisky was illegal. This would have been around 1938–1940. There was this one occasion I remember quite vividly. During this time, there were no Negro police in the South, and from time to time, the White police would drive through the neighborhood.

One day, Momma looked out the window and saw a police car drive past, and she said they were coming to the house. We had bought a gallon of whiskey the night before, because we had to buy at night, as it would decrease our chances of getting caught. I always went with her to buy the whiskey, and of course, at that age, I had no thoughts of our doing anything illegal, although Momma had told me so. To me, it was a matter of how we lived, bought food and clothing, and paid the few dollars a month rent to the "rent man," who was White of course.

She immediately poured the entire gallon of whiskey in the toilet and flushed it several times, so the rent money was literally flushed down the toilet!

The police officer did not come to our house.

Our house, 1110 West State Street, and the house at 1112 had our toilets on the back porch, which was covered by the tin roof and the closed wooden porch. The house around us to the south in which Willie lived, the one next door to him on the east side where Doris and Bernice lived, and the other house had outdoor toilets in small wooded stalls.

I do recall another event when a White police officer did come into the house and literally kicked Bud down the steps. I don't know the reason for the arrest, but I do remember that Colored men were arrested for being "drunk and disorderly."

We visited Bud at times as a member of the chain gang. This was a group of Colored men in orange over hall-like suits, chained at the ankles and working to lay rails for the trains that would sometime in the future run on them.

I am not sure when the concept of the Black Hawks came about. Jenk and Earl lived next door to each other on Dewitt Street, and several blocks west of their houses, across Beaver Street, was LaVilla Park. According to Wikipedia, LaVilla is located in Jacksonville, Florida, downtown, and is bordered by Beaver Street to the east and Adams Street to the west.

My recollection differs, at least for that time. LaVilla Park was several blocks west of our house and several blocks from State Street; further, Beaver Street was not Highway 95 at that time, but Kings Road (Highway 1) was.

It was the first suburb in Jacksonville. Originally, it was an independent city until it was annexed in 1887.

In 1821, Jacksonville was named after Andrew Jackson. The social activity was on Ashley Street, north of Broad Street, including Davis Street, and was the reason it was referred to as "the Harlem of the South." Several movie theaters were located on Ashley Street: the Strand Theater, which many considered the "top theater" for the Colored; the Frolic, farther north on Ashley Street; and the Roosevelt, which was the newest, at the end of Ashley and Davis Streets.

Bo Weaver, Bud's brother, and our Uncle William Beaver Calhoun, had a Bar and Pool Room on Ashley Street. Syl also had a café on Ashley Street, near the Frolic Theater. Many times, I would help clean the café. Later she closed the café and went into partnership with "a Cuban gentleman named Manuel," who owned Manuel's Tap Room on Ashley Street. She cooked and served the food and he the alcohol.

The Ritz Theater, the oldest, opened in 1929, and was located on Davis and State Streets, a block south of St. Pius Catholic School.

I spent many Saturdays at the Ritz watching cowboy movies, featuring the Lone Ranger, Red Ryder, and Wild Bill Hickok. This section of town, including LaVilla Park, is where we, the Black Hawks, would spend much of our fun time and early teenage years after school and on weekends.

Origin of the Black Hawks

The public school was across the street from the park on the north side, and there was a basketball court behind the school. For the guys, the basketball court, which was built on a cement surface, was the centerpiece of the action. This was the court on which the legend of the Black Hawks was born. The name, the Black Hawks, was taken from the comic book characters, the *Blackhawks*, a fictional name for a military group who fought the enemy wherever they encountered them. They first appeared in Military Comics, published by Quality Comics in 1941.

I do not know who decided on the name, but we all agreed to use it for our team in the summer of 1946. The park was on the west side of Beaver Street, a very busy street to cross, as there were no traffic lights in the area. Most of us rode our bikes to the park, and as I reflect, no one ever had concerns about our bikes being stolen. A softball diamond, makeshift really, with first base being near the fence, second base in the middle of the park, and third base to the east of the end of the basketball court, was where we played softball. Immediately behind the batter's box were tennis courts constructed of white sand, just as was found at the beach.

I recall one day during the summer, Jenk and I were playing basketball, and there were these two very pretty girls playing tennis. At that time, tennis was considered to be a "sissy sport" only played by girls. However, there were two brothers, "Leke and Deke"—Edward and David were their actual names—who also played. Furman Adams updated me as to his recollection of these early years. Furman was left handed and told me he played tennis along with Leke and Deke but stopped after he graduated from Stanton High School in 1953 and enrolled at FAMU in September 1954, the year I graduated.

America was at war with Korea at this time, and he said he was drafted into the U.S. Army.

On August 3, 1955, he and Yvonne, who lived on the same block, were married. They have been married for sixty-five years and had three children, two girls and a son.

After discharge from the army, he began work at the US Post Office in Jacksonville, where he spent thirty-five years before retiring.

Later, we would find that Everett "Chip" Reed, the playground director who played a significant role in my life (and about whom much will be said later), Charlie Parson, and General "Chappie" James, an air force pilot from Tuskegee Institute in Alabama, all Colored of course, often played tennis there. At that time, these were the only tennis courts Negroes could play on in Jacksonville.

At any rate, when Jenk and I saw these girls, we were duty bound to meet them. They were the Betsch sisters from the section of town called Sugar Hill, where the more well-to-do Negroes lived. One would later become the president of a very famous women's university in the South for Colored girls. There will be more about Sugar Hill later.

After we had watched them play for a while, because Jenk and I did not have tennis racquets, the four of us went to the small concession stand across from the courts. Jenk and I mixed some vanilla cookies, bananas, and Royal Crown Cola in two Tennis balls can they had. We offered some to them, but initially, they did not want any. However, they changed their minds and shared some with us. Jenk and I were invited to their home, and that was the first time and place we ever saw television (TV). It was black and white, as were all TVs at that time. This was in the summer of 1946. I cannot recall our paths ever crossing again.

Later, Jenk and I did get tennis racquets, and we began playing regularly. Occasionally, some of the adult men would also be playing on one of the adjacent courts.

At some point, "Chip" Reed, the playground director, took an interest in us. Chip would hit with us and gave us instructions on how to keep score, advised us never to cheat, and taught us other rules of the game. At that time, I improved at a faster pace than Jenk.

One day, Chip asked me about playing in a tournament. I was anxious to play, although I did not know what a tennis tournament was, and Momma would have to agree.

Chip came by the house one day during the summer of 1946. I would have been fourteen years old, turning fifteen on October 6, and he talked with Momma.

The Florida State Junior Championships for Negroes was being held in Daytona Beach, Florida, about forty miles from Jacksonville, and Chip asked if he could take me to the tournament. He told her he would take care of me and that we would not have to pay any money, which of course we did not have. I think I did have one tennis racquet I had bought from Irving's Sport Shop downtown, the only such sports shop in the city, using the money I had made from my paper routes. I also bought a pair of white Converse tennis shoes.

I must have had one or two pairs of white tennis shorts because white was the only color allowed for playing tennis. The only match I recall was playing the top seed in the finals.

We played on red clay courts, and I remember coming to the net very often. This strategy helped me to win. I do not recall what the scores were, but I won in two straight Sets.

My interest in tennis and confidence in my abilities were very much increased by this event.

The following year, I played in a junior tournament in West Palm Beach, Florida, with the opportunity to go the American Tennis Nationals (ATA) at Central State College in Ohio if I won. (More about the nationals later.)

I played Paul Bowie, now deceased, in the finals and lost. After the match, I found out that Paul was overage, which he knew, but he was selected to go to the Nationals. I had been raised not to cheat, so when I confronted Paul, he just laughed. I met Dr. E. Edgecombe, a surgeon at Howard University, now deceased, at this time and will speak more about him later. I believe I told him that one day I wanted to become

15

a surgeon. Paul, along with Jenk and I, enrolled at Florida Agricultural and Mechanical College (FAMC) and we did make the tennis team the freshman year.

After returning to FAMC after the Christmas break, we heard that Paul had drowned, a very disheartening event for all of us.

During our days of playing with the Black Hawks, Jenk and I would merge a lifelong relationship as best friends, much of it having to do with time spent playing on those two tennis courts and later courts throughout the country, but that is later on in the story!

I believe one of the reasons our team, the Black Hawks, became so dominant, is that we were all friends. I do not think any of us thought about or cared about one being "better" than the other; we just enjoyed playing basketball and being around each other.

Jenk, Earl (now deceased and about whom a postmortem piece will follow), and I spent a lot of time together. Jenk and Earl lived next door to each other on Dewitt Street, and during the days when the weather was inclement or we could not play outside, we played checkers and bid whiz, usually in Earl's house.

I always enjoyed going over to their houses because they had electricity and indoor toilets as I previously mentioned; moreover, at that time, Bill and I did not stay together all of the time, so there were more people to play with.

The Black Hawks would disband after the summer of 1948, the year we won the citywide basketball tournament. (Note the copy of the award given in1951 on the book cover.)

Earl would graduate from Stanton High School in Jacksonville, the only high school for Negroes at that time in January 1949 and would go off to the Kentucky State College for Negroes as it was known then, in Frankfurt, Kentucky. It became Kentucky State University in 1972.

I would meet Earl again on September of 1959 at Meharry Medical College in Nashville, Tennessee, where I was starting as a freshman medical student, and he was a graduating senior. Earl was a lifesaver, in as much as he gave me his microscope, which was a requirement for freshmen, and my finances were meager, to say the least. He also gave me very important advice on how to negotiate the four years at Meharry.

There will be more discussion about this later.

I was very socially and emotionally immature during those early years ending in June of 1949 when I graduated from Stanton High School. I was fifteen and would not reach sixteen until my birthday on October 6. Emotionally, my senior year was centered on my infatuation with Trudy (she has given me verbal permission to use her name), one of the prettiest girls in our class at Stanton.

I stayed at St. Pius for the tenth grade and started Stanton for the eleventh and twelfth grades. My problem was shyness! At that time, I was not confident enough to sit up front in my classes, even though I always made good grades, mostly A's and B's. Eventually, the time approached to get a date for the senior prom. Although I really wanted to go with Trudy, I did not have the nerve to ask her, so I asked another girl with whom I could talk about almost anything, never feeling shy. I remember she said yes she would go with me, and I believe she was very happy. This would have been around the beginning of the week because prom night was on Friday.

To my absolute unbelief, a few days later, Trudy asked me to take her to the prom! (By the way, I did talk with Trudy in 2020 by phone. She is living in Martha's Vineyard. She gave me permission to use her name.) I think it was on a Wednesday. This was a dream come true; the one person I was completely infatuated with (I am sure this was at the age of the puppy love stage) asked me to take her to the prom!

Gleefully, I said yes, but I knew in my heart that was not right because I had already asked another girl, and she said yes. Somehow, I told the girl I had asked that I could not take her.

I asked my uncle Drew, Syl's younger brother, who had a car, to take Trudy and me to the prom and pick us up, which he did. Although on one level, I was overjoyed to be going to the prom with Trudy, it was a bittersweet joy, because I knew I had offended the other young lady. It was not my nature to knowingly offend anyone. I cannot recall if she and I ever had a conversation after that, and why would she? Since the prom was the last event except for the graduation, I do not recall ever seeing her again.

I had very little money during those days and had only a bike for transportation. That was the only time Trudy and I would "date." Graduation was the following week, and that was the last time I saw Trudy for a while. That fall, she would enter Howard University in September

1949. I did see her again in December 1962 when my roommate and I drove to Detroit, Michigan, to see his girlfriend. I went along to help him drive.

We were in our senior year of medical school at Meharry Medical College in Nashville, Tennessee, and would graduate as physicians in May 1963.

Detroit was the coldest place I had ever been. The temperature was in the minus degrees as I recall. I cannot remember the circumstances of how Trudy and I would happen to meet on that particular evening. I did not know anything about her personal life at that time, nor she mine, but I remember I asked her to marry me!

How dumb was that? I had not seen her in over ten years, and to come up with a question like "Will you marry me?" Of course she said no, with a kind smile, I am sure. She said she had finished her training as a Nurse in Anesthesiology and was engaged at that time.

Some years later, she and her husband visited with Shirley and me here in DC. The circumstances of this visit I thought were interesting. It seems that she and her husband were at a party being given by a tennis-playing friend of ours, Ben Metz, now deceased. (He gave me verbal permission to use his name before he died.) Apparently, their conversation involved tennis.

As the story goes, Trudy had indicated she knew someone in her hometown of Jacksonville, Florida, who played tennis, Tommy Calhoun. Ben and I had known each other through tennis for over ten years at this point, and in fact, he had helped me financially when I was in medical school. After medical school, I started my practice as a General Surgeon here in DC. We became partners in opening a tennis shop here in DC, the first tennis shop owned by Negroes. Unfortunately, after about six months, we had to close because of lack of business.

Ben called me on the phone, and to my absolute surprise, the next voice was Trudy's! We talked for about ten minutes. The next day, she and her husband did come and visit with Shirley and me at our home at 4010 Argyle Terrace, NW. (More about 4010 later.)

The summer of 1949, I had graduated from Stanton. Jenk and I would spend a lot of time playing tennis. As I noted earlier, the tennis courts at LaVilla Park were sand courts, the same as the white sand at the local seashores (beaches), so one can easily imagine what they looked like after one slide. It left a big hole. The Department of Recreation would roll and reline the courts twice a month, so those of us who had a keen interest in playing tennis knew those dates well.

At that time, there were no other tennis courts in Jacksonville where we, the Coloreds, could play. Later, two cement courts would be constructed at Wilder Park, a section of Sugar Hill.

In 1927, the Jacksonville Public Library was also located in Sugar Hill, the area in Jacksonville where the most prominent Negroes lived, as I noted previously.

In the 1930s, descendants of Charles B. Wilder, a Colored entrepreneur, donated thirty acres of land in the area, and a Community Center was developed.

The tennis courts were constructed in the 1940s in the area called Wilder Park.

Another young lady we met was R. E., and most of her tennis was played at Wilder Park (see photo and newspaper article). She was an up-and-coming junior player with whom we lost touch after we left Jacksonville for FAMC in Tallahassee.

Most of Sugar Hill and the Wilder Park Community was demolished as the city claimed "the right of domain" of the area in 1958 to make room for Interstate Highway 95.

It is reported in Wikipedia that, "Perhaps Sugar Hill (sh) was a little too nice for Jim Crow Jacksonville".

(sh) https://www.moderncities.com>articles>2017-feb-lost.

I soon got a job, newspaper routes in the morning and evening. The *Jacksonville Journal* was the afternoon paper and the *Florida Times Union*, the morning paper. Jenk and I both delivered the *Jacksonville Journal*, and we usually met at the LaVilla Tennis Courts in the afternoon around 4:30 to 5:00 p.m. after we finished delivering our newspapers.

The highlight of this summer was the trip Jenk and I and another boy whose name I cannot recall won to Havana, Cuba. The previous summer of 1948, he and I and another boy whose name I cannot recall had won a trip to Washington DC and New York City. Each of these trips was the prize awarded because we three boys recruited the highest number of new subscribers to the *Jacksonville Journal*, the afternoon newspaper.

In Washington DC, I remember we walked up the stairs to the top of the Washington Monument and back down to the street.

In New York, we stayed at the Theresa Hotel, a famous hotel where Negroes stayed, and I remember talking with Fidel Castro, who was a guest at the hotel.

What I recall mostly about the trip to Havana was getting seasick, although I did not know what that was at the time. I was standing on the deck of the ship looking at the beautiful blue-green water and waves, and all of a sudden, I felt dizzy and wanted to throw up.

I went back to my room and felt better after a while.

CHAPTER 2
THE MIDDLE YEARS

The middle years for me started in the summer of 1949. I was sixteen and had graduated from Stanton High School in June. We knew there was no money for me to go to college. Stanton for me was two years because I attended from September 1947 to June 1949 in grades eleven and twelve. I spent the tenth grade at St. Pius, a trial year to see if there were enough interest and resources for it to become a high school. There were not, so the tenth grade was not offered the following year.

There were five boys, the Brown brothers, Allen, Forrest, and me.

I cannot remember all of the girls' names, but I do remember Betty R. was the smartest in our group. She and I usually alternated as to who won the most gold stars in the spelling bees.

As previously noted, then White Nuns from the Sisters` of Saint Joseph and two White Priests` ran the school and taught most of the classes. One of the Priests taught Latin, which became one of my favorite classes.

There was one Colored lady, whom we called "the lady of a thousand faces" because she was frequently contorting her face for emphasis. She taught mathematics in the sixth and seventh grades.

I was "skipped" from grade four to five and again from six to seven, which was often done during this time if a student was thought to be very bright. Momma, Syl, and I were very excited about this, but years later, that practice was abandoned in favor of adding "advanced courses" for the "bright" student to take.

From my perspective, now, I realize that I was still very immature and slow in developing social skills, which thankfully I did correct as I got older.

I graduated from Stanton in June of 1949.

When the school year started in September 1949, I was a bit sad because I could not go to College, and my days were no longer structured as they were during a school year.

Jenk started his senior year in high school, and I continued work delivering newspapers in the morning and afternoons. We were able to play tennis and basketball in the afternoons.

Sometime during the fall, September or October, I got a job at the King Edward's Cigar Factory and began work as a busboy and helping Charles (the Cook) in the kitchen. The pay was more than I made from the two paper routes.

From time to time, he would let me make some of the sandwiches. My hours were from 7:00 a.m. to 3:00 p.m. I rode my bike to and from the factory, about three to five miles each way.

In hindsight, I am sure that is one reason I was in good physical shape. At that age, I don't think I ever got tired from playing basketball or tennis.

Jenk and I would meet in the afternoons at the LaVilla Park Tennis Courts. We were both planning to go to Florida Agricultural and Mechanical College (FAMC) as it was called at that time and hoped to play on the tennis team.

As I noted earlier, I was very disappointed that I could not go to college after graduating from Stanton when most of my classmates went off to colleges somewhere. Of course, the reason I did not go was because we did not have any money for me to go. On the positive side, I had earned an academic scholarship, the Lewis State Scholarship, worth $200, for those who would become teachers in the state of Florida, so I could look forward to it taking care of some of my expenses.

At the time, I was not fully aware of the requirement to teach in the state if I accepted the scholarship. According to Google, it appears that the Scholarship Act of 1949, cosponsored by J. Lewis Hall, provided the funds to Florida A & M College for academically oriented students. The funds were a percentage of winnings from horse racing in the state of Florida.

I did save some money from my job, and I had a suit, grey and white on a dark-green background, tailor-made for twenty-five dollars. The suit was ready the week before I would leave for Tallahassee, Florida, and FAMC. I also had a pair of Converse tennis shoes, two Jack Kramer wood tennis racquets, and a pair of black dress shoes, along with shirts and underwear and several pair of pants. I am sure I had a winter coat, although winters in Florida had temperatures around 50 degrees Fahrenheit, and no lower than forty degrees.

I do remember the first snow I saw was in Tallahassee during that first winter.

School stared in September of 1950, and after having been away from the academic environment for over a year, I was eager for the excitement and challenges of FAMC.

Florida Agricultural and Mechanical College was located in Tallahassee, Florida, about 185 miles away, in the far northwest corner of the state. The only other cities in the state I had visited were Marianna, Saint Augustine, Daytona Beach, where I won the Junior State Championship in 1948; and West Palm Beach, where I played in another tennis tournament. I was fifteen years old that summer.

As I recall, my brother, Bill, and I had spent two summers in Marianna, Florida, where I was born, several years earlier on the farm of Momma's brother, Uncle Pilot.

Those summers consisted of our getting up at 5:00 a.m. and going with our older cousins to "pick cotton and peanuts" in the fields. We would also walk behind our cousins while they plowed. We would stop for a great breakfast and go back into the fields until sundown. After we returned to the house and washed up, we always had great dinners.

On one occasion, Bill and I caught a turtle and gave it to our aunt, Pilot's wife, and she made turtle stew. It was the first and only time I can remember having eaten turtle stew … and it was good!

The second summer we visited, I was a year older, perhaps twelve years old, and one day, I was riding one of the horses, bareback, as there were no saddles. I was galloping along when suddenly the horse stopped, and I went headfirst over his head! His head struck my mouth and dislodged an upper tooth. Many years later, the tooth had to be pulled because it had become darkened in color.

Anatomically, it was a Central Incisor.

CHAPTER 3
THE COLLEGE YEARS

Freshman Year

Freshman year was mostly about my adjustment and getting over a crushing heartbreak!

The first week, I met B, as I will call her. I thought she was even prettier than Trudy. She had soft chocolate-colored skin and was about five feet four or five. She was from Orlando, Florida.

We met on a Monday, and by Friday, she had dumped me for a junior. I was crushed!

It took me several months to recover, although my grades did not suffer at all, and I did have my tennis.

Further, I continued to attend Sunday Mass at the Catholic Church in the city. We had to take a bus, and of course, the Coloreds had to sit in the back. There were not very many of us from FAMC who attended Mass. Two years later, a Catholic Church would be built near the college campus.

Jenk, who also entered FAMC at that time, and I did make the tennis team as the number-three doubles team. I was the number-five singles player, and he was number six.

Sometime during that first semester, we went to a National Intercollegiate Athletic Association (NIAA)–sponsored tennis and track and field event in Abilene, Texas. North Carolina A & T and Prairie View were the other Colored schools invited.

He and I won our doubles match, but both of us lost our singles matches.

My Singles match still stands out in my mind. I had won the first set against my White opponent, and I was leading five-love in the second set, when two White girls sat down on a bench to watch our match. I looked over and saw them and proceeded to lose every game from then on, losing the match, 3-6, 7-5, 6-0!

Remember, I was a Colored boy from the South, and I had never had any distance relationship with White girls—not that this was a relationship!

I did pledge for the Alpha Phi Alpha Fraternity, which was the academically oriented fraternity for men on campus. Among the many events that occurred during my pledging was the indignity I felt when the junior James B., as I will call him (he was an Alpha and the guy who stole my first flame, B) had me doing some ridiculous tasks.

Ironically, nineteen years later, Shirley, my wife, and our child were living at 54 G Street South West in DC, and one afternoon, I was jogging around the large field near the house when whom do I see but James B.? We recognized each other and had a brief but pleasant conversation … I don't remember any details of the discussion.

At the time, for some reason, he seemed different from what I recalled, and it dawned on me that when we first met, I was sixteen years old, and nineteen years later, I had outgrown him physically!

Another event during "hell week" was having to appear at the window of Alfred F., the dean of pledgees, at 6:00 a.m. and recite for him the entire *Rubaiyat of Omar Khayyam* by Rudyard Kipling (1865–1936).

I would recall some of those verses later on in my life as difficult circumstances would arise.

"If you can keep your head about you while those about are losing theirs and blaming it on you but make allowances for their doubting too; if you can wait and not be tired of waiting, or being lied about and don't deal in lies, or being hated, don't give way to hating, and yet don't look too good, nor talk too wise; if you can walk with crowds and keep your virtue or walk with Kings nor lose the common touch; if neither foes nor loving friends can hurt you; if you can fill the unforgiving minute with sixty seconds' worth of distance run—yours is the Earth and everything that is in it, and which is more—you'll be a Man my Son."

Syl sent me the sixty-five dollars needed to complete my initiation, and I "crossed the burning sands" to become a member of the Alpha Phi Alpha Fraternity.

My grades overall were good except the grade "C" I was given in tennis. The physical education teacher was a very beautiful young lady who did not play tennis, nor could she teach it, in my opinion. Even so, my grade point average the freshman year was 2.4 on a 3.0 system.

One of the great experiences I had during my freshman and sophomore years at FAMC was knowing one of the students, Althea Gibson, who graduated in 1952.

During my sophomore year, I was fortunate enough to have practiced tennis with Althea, and in fact, I won three games in the two sets we played. She would play a significant role later as I will note.

She played on the women's basketball team and was an outstanding player. At that time, by women's rules, the whole team could not run the entire court, but each team had one player who could play the entire floor. Althea was the player for FAMU, the school now having become a university.

Another thing about her was her pool-shooting ability. Often, she would come to the men's dorm rec room in the basemen and shoot pool, usually besting most of the guys.

Redlining

I think the pool room was Jenk's downfall because I frequently had to tell him he should leave the pool room and get his studies done. Being away from home for the first time with no one to answer to was more than a challenge for some, as it was for Jenk.

The school had a very cruel system, I thought, of posting first-semester exam grades of freshmen outside of the dining room, *redlining* those who had failed.

One of those names was Jenk's!

Another time in the future, I experienced *redlining*. During my first year in medical school, one of the major courses was Physiology, and after the midterm exam, all grades were posted outside of the laboratory. Those who failed had their names posted and *redlined*.

At FAMU, those who failed were dismissed. In medical school, some were allowed to repeat the first year. I never did find out how that determination was made.

Jenk did not make good grades at that time, and he left after the first semester and enlisted in the Air Force for four years. We kept in touch over the years periodically with letters.

I remember his telling me he would often spend hours hitting tennis balls against a wall (something Arthur Ashe did at an early age), and that would help him become the best Black male tennis player in the country during the years of 1956 through 1958, except for Arthur Ashe, and our becoming the best Black men's doubles players during the same period.

We would spend some time together in 1955 after his discharge from the air force, which is described later in "The Reunion." (See also the newspaper article.)

I was a first lieutenant in the army by that time, stationed at Fort Meade, Maryland. On one occasion, I recall we were driving from DC for a tennis tournament in Baltimore. I was in my uniform, and he wanted to drive. We were speeding along at 70 miles an hour, and a White police officer passed us, looked over at us, smiled, and drove on. I could see us being pulled over and my being reported as an army officer for speeding; the speed limit was sixty miles per hour.

I knew I needed to get a job the summer of 1950 after my freshman year. I was fortunate enough to get a job at the Jacksonville Shipyard, making good money for a Colored man during this time.

My foreman was a White male whom I will refer as "Mr. Dale A."

My job was scraping barnacles from the hull of the ship. Barnacles are small parasites, marine crustaceans, unlike crabs or shrimp, and many would become permanently attached to the hulls. They develop chitinous, or hard, calcified surfaces, and my job was to scrape these surfaces clean. In Jacksonville, in the summer, the temperatures were always in the mid-90 degrees, so after a short time down in the hull, I was sweating as though I were in a sauna. Periodically, Mr. Dale A. would look down into the hull to see how or what I was doing.

He also had me cleaning from under the house of the wife of one of the ship owners. Although this was under the house, it was a step up from the inside of the hulls of the ships.

I am sure I made up my mind then and there that in the future, I was *not* going to work for a White boss but work for myself.

A stabilizing force for me then, as it has been up to this point in my life, was my Catholic faith. At that time in Tallahassee, there was one Catholic Church in town that we Colored Catholics could attend, but we had to sit on the back row of seats or stand. We were the last to receive Holy Communion.

There was the opportunity to go to Confession and receive the sacrament of Penance, which we believe not only absolves us of our sins in God's eye but also strengthens us against the tendency toward conceit and arrogance, enhancing the tendency toward humility. This was also afforded us on Saturday afternoons.

Freshman year was mostly about adjusting to being away from home and making good grades. I believe I always enjoyed learning and reading during my early years. As pledgees in Alpha Phi Alpha Fraternity, we were encouraged to make the best grades we could.

Sophomore Year

I was happy to get back to college at FAMC in September, although I did feel a bit sad in leaving Momma, who lived alone. She was working now, five days a week at the New York Laundry downtown.

On some occasions, I would go to meet her, and we would stop by the Cohen Brothers' Department Store to buy some clothes for me to take back to college.

I still have flashbacks of the two faucets for drinking water in front of the store, one for "Whites only" and the other for the Colored. Sometimes, when I did not think anyone would see me, I drank from that White faucet, and it seemed like the same water to me!

The job was a blessing for Momma, because it was a good social outlet as well as a means for support.

Tom Calhoun (Bud), her husband after whom I was named, had left to go "up north" sometime in the summer of 1949 to Wilmington, Delaware, to find work. I think they were legally married, but I am not sure, as there were a number of common-law relationships among the Coloreds and the Whites during those times. This was during the Depression and post-Depression years, and well-paying jobs were hard to find, especially for Negroes. Bud was about six feet tall, I think, and had dark-brown skin. I do not remember him talking much around the house at 1110 West State Street. I do not ever remember him saying an unkind word or cursing or ever being violent to Momma or me. I was told they had twins, but both died just after birth, and they had no other children. It was not uncommon at that time among Negroes for large families to give one or two of the children to other Colored families who did not have children. This was especially helpful to the family with no children because help was needed on the farms.

I was given to live with Bud and Luella, as I would understand later, because Syl, my birth mother, was not married and very young at the time, and unable to support us. There are several events in my life involving Bud that do come to mind.

The first occurred when I was around nine or ten years old. I had gone to a movie about Frankenstein and the Wolf Man. I must have awakened during the night screaming and trying to leave the house because they were "coming to get me"! Bud came to me, calmed me down, and told me I was dreaming. Another time, he and I had gone fishing and were walking along a wooden plank when I saw a fish. I reached down, picked it up, and threw it away, screaming because I thought it was a snake.

Bud told me it was an eel, and that night, we had eel for dinner. Bud worked for the Seaboard Airline Railroad as a laborer, which was a very good job for Negroes. One perk was that we, his immediate family, could ride in the last car of the train for free, wherever the train went. I recall we had some very good fried chicken lunches as we took a few trips to Marianna, Florida, to visit with Momma's brother Pilot and his family and to Savannah, Georgia, to visit with Momma's sister. I do not remember her name.

Negroes could not eat in the dining car, although only Negroes served the food and drinks, and worked as Pullman Porters.

For those Social Historians, the unionization of Pulman Cars under the direction of A. Phillip Randolph would make interesting reading.

Bud had an accident at some point, severely injuring a leg, and I remember visiting him at Brewster's Hospital. I would have been about eight or nine years old at the time.

The next time I visited Brewster's Hospital was in 1965, when Momma had been taken there.

I remember holding her hand and saying to her, "Momma, this is Tommy!"

She uttered a few monosyllabic sounds, squeezed my hand, and died.

Syl had found her on the floor at 1110 West State Street. No cause of death was recorded. It was assumed she had a stroke.

She had been living alone again then because Bud, who did come back to Jacksonville, had died.

I was in the third year of my surgery residency in Norfolk, Virginia, at the time, so after three days and the funeral, I had to return to Norfolk.

I do not believe Momma had any kind of relationship with any other man than Bud, and I often wondered how she spent her evenings and weekends. I am sure I prayed regularly for her, as well as for Syl and Bill. By then, Syl and Bill were living on Myrtle Avenue in a very nice place with electricity and inside toilets. Their house was near the baseball park where the Negro Baseball League played their games.

At some point, I remember Henry "Hank" Aaron was in town, and as I recall, I went to some of the games.

FAMC Changed to FAMU

At a noon conference in 1953, the name Florida Agricultural and Mechanical College was changed to Florida Agricultural and Mechanical University (FAMU). This was quite an historical milestone, and even today, FAMU is well established among higher-learning institutions. The FAMU Rattler football team, with its legendary coach "Jake Gaither," was the scourge of the football world among the Negro college campuses.

The Florida A&M marching band was also getting regional and national recognition under the direction of Dr. Foster, now deceased.

Before I graduated, the word was that A&M's band was second only to the Michigan State band. I would get my orange-and-green sports jacket as a member of the tennis team in September of 1951.

My sophomore year would be one of the best years of my life.

I had been accepted into the Reserve Officers' Training Corp (ROTC) in my freshman year, so I needed to be sure my grades were good because starting the junior year, ROTC students made fifty dollars a month! I could not wait!

One event that merits noting occurred during the first semester of my sophomore year.

There was going to be a professional tennis match in Jacksonville in October 1951 (not sure about the month) featuring Jack Kramer, Richard "Pancho" Gonzales, Frank Sedgman from Australia, and Francisco "Pancho" Segura from South America, the leading professional tennis players in the world. The professional tennis tour was in its infancy, and Jacksonville, Florida, was one of the first stops on the tour. Mr. Lee Pennington, now deceased, the math professor and tennis enthusiast at FAMU, had agreed to take some of us on the tennis team to see the match in Jacksonville, about 185 miles from Tallahassee.

When we reached the arena for the event, Jack Kramer, the number-one professional men's singles player was warming up with Pancho Gonzales from California for their match. When our group, the four of us Negroes, approached the door, we were told that we could not enter. I spoke up very loudly and asked why, as we had the ticket money, and all we wanted to do was see the matches.

Pancho Gonzales apparently overheard our loud talking, looked over, and told the White guy that he would *not* play if we were *not* let in!

They did find a spot for us near the back but with a pretty good view, and we were able to watch the matches.

We drove back to campus that same night, very happy that we could see some of the best tennis players in the world that evening!

National Intercollegiate Championships

I stayed for summer school after my sophomore year as did Dave Geiger, who was also from Jacksonville. Because I had been on the Lewis State Academic Scholarship, there were certain credits I needed, which I had not taken. We took Typing and Art History. We were the only two males in the classes, which meant there were special incentives, and we made A's in both.

The summer after my sophomore year, the American Tennis Association (ATA) National Championships were to be held in Daytona Beach, Florida, so after summer school, I was able to go. Unfortunately, I had not been able to practice much because of summer school, but I went anyway.

One of the most blessed events in my life would occur at the tournament! I had lost my singles match in a close match to an older, top-seeded player, after having the match point. I tried a drop shot, which he was able to reach, and I lost that point and the match.

During this time, the National Intercollegiate Singles Championships for Negro Colleges was being held at the same time. FAMU did not have a representative in the tournament, and someone—I have no idea who—apparently told the committee that Tom Calhoun from FAMU was at the tournament. I was contacted and told that I could play, representing FAMU.

I would beat DeWitt Willis from North Carolina A&T in the semifinals and Ron Charity from Virginia Union (the person who introduced Arthur Ashe to tennis, now deceased) in the finals. Later that day, I found some quiet time to say some prayers of thanksgiving because I *never* had any thoughts of playing in the intercollegiate event, much less of winning the singles championship!

Junior Year

I started my junior year in September 1953. It was a transforming period in many respects.

During the first two weeks after school had started in September, there was a noonday ceremony, recognizing me as the new intercollegiate singles champion (see the picture of Coach Austin giving me the trophy). My campus status was much improved!

Moreover, beginning in October, we in the Reserve Officers' Training Corps (ROTC) began receiving our monthly checks of fifty dollars. I was Captain of the tennis team and the number-one player, so with regular monthly funds, I could go on a date more often and keep a fresh pack of filtered Kent cigarettes, all of which would make me more of a man about campus!

By this time, I was becoming more self-confident. I had a solo singing role in a play and was more active in student body activities. I had a full tennis scholarship for my junior and senior years, which meant free room and board. Also, as Captain of the tennis team, Coach provided me two new tennis McGregor tennis racquets.

My junior year was a good year. I maintained good grades, and to my surprise and delight, although I tried to remain cool, several of the campus beauties were themselves starting more conversations with me. As I reflect on those days, I am very thankful to the good Lord because I continued to go Mass every Sunday, although I should have gone to Confession more often.

Reserve Officers' Training Corps (ROTC) at Fort Bliss, Texas

The big event for the summer that those of us in the ROTC were looking forward to was our trip to Fort Bliss, Texas, just outside of El Paso, Texas. The school year as a junior ROTC officer meant drilling and training with our M-16 rifles, which were never loaded. I was made a Captain, which meant I had command of two Platoons of men, each Platoon having twelve members. Two Platoons constituted a Battery. We had to practice precision drills on a regular basis, and periodically, when the entire Battalion of men assembled, each battery commander had to sound off with a loud, clear voice, identifying his battery. My sound off was for Battery A. "Attention!" (*atten … shun!*). Then I would give a crisp hand salute to the Battalion Commander, who was Harry B. At Fort Bliss, we were joined by other ROTC members from other schools, such as North Carolina A&T and Hampton.

Integrated Dance

I recall graduation from summer camp was fast approaching, and we had heard that there was always a graduation dance, but in the past, the Colored ROTC officers often did not attend because there were no Colored women. Several of us got together and decided that we should present our concern to the commanding officer, a White Colonel, that we wanted to go to the dance, but there were no Colored women with whom we could dance. I was elected to present our case to the colonel. Officer Calhoun, shoes shined, uniform pressed, presented himself and sharply saluted the Colonel. In summary, I told him we, the Colored officers, wanted to go to the dance but would not be able to dance with anyone. I indicated that of course we would act as officers and gentlemen.

I don't remember if he asked me any questions, and I was dismissed. Back at the dormitory, I told the guys about the meeting, but the Colonel did not give me an answer. Nearby was Texas Western College in El Paso. It was an all-White college.

On the day of the dance, word came that since the dance would be held on the military base, we could ask the young ladies to dance. We had decided we go as a group and leave as a group about forty-five minutes before the dance would end.

Guess who was the only one who did not ask for a dance?

Yup, me!

I am not sure if it was because I was still somewhat bashful or if I thought the White officers would be out to get me since they thought I was the leader.

I watched as many of the guys danced and seem to have fun, many fantasizing, I am sure, as I did, of some wistful tryst!

I think I told the guys later that I was just not up to dancing that evening or some other nonsense! There were no negative issues thereafter, and we all finished the summer ROTC program in good standing. At this time, Texas Western College was still a College for Whites only.

First Integrated National Basketball Championships

Fast-forward to March 16, 1966, the all-Colored men's basketball team from Texas Western College defeated the all-White University of Kentucky team, which was ranked number one in the country, 72 to 65 in the historic National Championship game, played at Cole's Field House in College Park, Maryland.

After that game, more Colleges and Universities began slowly recruiting Colored players.

Texas Western College is now the University of Texas at El Paso (UTEP).

Another interesting event occurred during this time. My roommate, whose name I cannot recall, was from Hampton University in Hampton, Virginia. I was assigned to Battery A, which was the same assignment I had had during my senior year at FAMU, as well as during the summer of 1953 at El Paso, Texas, during ROTC training.

Midway through the first six weeks, we had the first exam, and I earned the highest grade of all the schools. My room mate who did not make a very good grade broke out in tears, thinking he would not graduate. I tried to console him, noting this was just the first exam, and over-all performance would likely determine who would graduate.

I found out later that my making the highest score, caused somewhat of a stir among the class. Directly across from our dormitory room were two White students from Princeton University. We were not given much respect as Colored officers, but after the grades were posted, one of the guys from Princeton became somewhat friendly with me.

This was a shaky relationship at best, because a trash can from their room went missing, and I recalled he looked into our room to see if we had taken it. Of course we had not!

All the rooms were unlocked, and daily weekday inspections were carried out by senior officers, making sure our bunks (beds) were crisply made up each morning, our shoes were carefully aligned, there was no dust present, and essentially, all was well ordered. They wore white gloves and rubbed all surfaces to see if dust was present.

There was an unpleasant event that sticks out in my mind.

Threat!

One day, Harry B., who was the Battalion Commander of our ROTC class at FAMU, and another of our classmates came to my room … when my roommate was not there.

They essentially threatened me!

Harry told me he was planning on being the outstanding student from FAMU!

I had been performing very well in the field, and my earning the highest mark on that first exam, I surmised, posed a threat to Harry.

I think I almost found it laughable, and I told Harry I was not interested in an army career. Harry was planning on an army career, and I suppose he felt I would somehow impede his goals. I never had the desire for an army career, and after I told him so, this apparently satisfied him, as there were no further incidents.

I had some thoughts about reporting this to our commanding officer, but I kind of felt sorry for Harry, who was not known for a stellar academic performance a FAMU. I dismissed the incident, and during our senior year, there was never any discussion about it.

Foot Fault Call by Althea Gibson

The most disappointing event I can recall happened at the end of my junior year when Althea Gibson, the chair umpire for the finals match, called a "foot fault" on me!

I was defending the National Intercollegiate Singles Championship that I had won in the summer of 1952 against Julius "June Bug" Martin, from North Carolina A&T in Daytona Beach, Florida.

We were in the fifth set at five-all, and I was serving at "ad out" when the foot fault was called!

I was freaked out that I had lost that game on a foot fault, and June Bug won his serve to win the match 7-5!

I do not know what happened to June Bug, and I never saw him at any of the future tennis tournaments.

Senior Year

Senior year just seemed to fly past. My biggest challenge was Physics.

I just never could seem to grasp the concepts, though I devoted a ton of time to studying. The best grade I could get was a D+. It was the only time in my entire academic life I ever got a D. I was really upset because I thought it would prevent me from being able to go into medical school when the time came to apply.

I was popular about the campus and ran for the title of "King of the campus." I did not campaign for the title, and a football player was named king. I did take the campus Queen to the senior prom, however, and we later became friends, along with her husband and my wife, Shirley. We would meet again some years later in Washington DC.

The campus Queen would also become the National President of the Delta Sigma Delta Sorority, of which Shirley was also a member.

During my senior year, I was elected Vice President of our class. Shannon, who became a general in the army, was President. I was elected the Dean of Pledgees for the fraternity Alpha Phi Alpha and, as such, lived in the "frat room," alone my senior year.

Of course, the room was always busy with some fraternity activity.

The tennis team did well, as Roosevelt Thomas (now deceased), Chet Miles (now with Parkinson's disease), and I made up the nucleus of the team.

Looking back, I see I did not want the college years to end. Sometime earlier, as I noted previously, a small Catholic Church had been built near the campus for the Coloreds, so that I never missed Sunday Mass, and I think I went to Confession more often.

Graduation was bittersweet. It was four years of growth and maturation of mind, body, and spirit. There were good times and bad times. Although looking back, I wonder how bad were they really? I got over my first love rejection before my freshman first semester was over. The pain of being paddled while crossing the burning sand was immediately forgotten when I became a member of the Alpha Phi Alpha fraternity.

There was not much I can recall about my sophomore year, but the summer after that year was when I won the National Intercollegiate Tennis Singles, representing FAMU in Daytona Beach, Florida, as I previously noted. I did lose one singles match to a player from Prairie View Agricultural and Mechanical College (A&M) when they come to play us at FAMU in 1954.

Prairie View is now a member of Texas A&M University and is the second largest of the historically Black colleges and universities (HBCU) in Texas with over 9,500 students.

My junior and senior years were mostly positive, with growth intellectually, spiritually, and physically, and I was blessed with good health.

Syl, my biological mother, came to graduation, and that was a real joy for both of us. I think we rode the train back to Jacksonville.

Back home in Jacksonville, the summer after graduation was short-lived. I was scheduled to report for active duty as a newly appointed Second Lieutenant in the US Army at Fort Bliss, Texas, in El Paso, Texas, on September 28, 1954.

CHAPTER 4
ATLANTIC CITY, NEW JERSEY

Dave Geiger and I had made plans to go Atlantic City, New Jersey, to work and party the summer after graduation. Dave had been dismissed by Sergeant F. from the ROTC program for reasons neither he nor I could understand.

Later, Dave would go to veterinary school in Tuskegee, Alabama, and after graduation, would join the US Army as a Captain.

We rode the Greyhound bus from Jacksonville, Florida, to Atlantic City, New Jersey, in early June 1954, the summer after graduation. I had saved a little money from my last ROTC check, and I am sure Momma and Syl gave me some money as well. Dave had some money of his own. Neither Dave nor I had been to Atlantic City, but we had heard about it being a fun-filled place during the summer, and we felt confident we would find work.

Upon arrival, we got a room in the Young Men's Christian Association (YMCA or Y) for Negroes for seven dollars a week. I had the top bunk bed, reminding me of my freshmen year in College when I had a top bunk bed in the men's dormitory.

For some reason I thought of my roommate my junior year at FAMU, Alvin White, now deceased, who earned a Master of Arts degree from Columbia University in New York and his Doctor of Education Degree from Northern Virginia (NOVA) South Eastern University in Ft. Lauderdale, Florida. He became the first Black principal of a predominately White school, Robert E. Lee, High School, and the first Black principal of the predominately White but now integrated Ribault Senior High School in

Jacksonville, Florida. He later would serve as assistant superintendent for desegregation of public schools. (See *Education Is NOT a Four-Letter Word*, a book by Dr. Alvin G. White, First Edition Copyright 2008, Library of Congress.)

In November of 2007, I went back to Jacksonville for a visit to St. Vincent's, a large Catholic Hospital as part of my physician consulting work for Providence Hospital here in Washington DC. Alvin, Jamie, my next-door neighbor from 1112 West State Street, and I had dinner one evening. It was the first time in fifty years we had seen each other. We each mused that since we still recognized each other at least dementia had not set in so far. We had a great time recalling old times that evening and a great meal at Red Lobster.

The first two weeks in Atlantic City were not good for me in that I would not find a job. Dave had found work, though I cannot recall what he was doing. I had met a very pretty young lady working as a waitress in a nearby café, so when I was not job hunting, I often went there for a cup of coffee and a slice of apple pie, ten cents for the coffee and twenty-five cents for the apple pie. Some evenings, we would sit on her steps talking. She lived close to the Y.

The hit musical song that year was "Hey There" by Sammy Davis Jr., and occasionally, when I went to the café, I splurged, put a quarter in the jukebox, and played that song.

Northern Racism

Most of my job hunting was visiting hotels in the business area of Atlantic City. After about two weeks, I did get a job as a "handyman" in what would now be a three-star hotel, owned by a Jewish lady. I recall it was about four to five stories high, and I had to make sure all the rooms were clean and fresh linen was available.

Most of the rooms were unoccupied. There was an occasion that remains fixed in my mind. A young Colored female came into the office one day and asked if there were any rooms available. To my absolute amazement, the owner told her, "I'm sorry, we are completely filled," which was an absolute lie! The owner presented a very pleasant appearance in turning her away, and this was my firsthand experience with Northern racism.

I was able to play tennis on a regular basis on the hard courts in the city. I found some red clay courts in Ashbury, New Jersey, a sort of suburb in Atlantic City, and on several occasions, I took the bus to and from those courts. I did meet a pretty good player there, and we arranged to meet once a week to play.

Some fifty years later, Jenk and I were playing doubles at the Four Seasons Tennis Club in Fairfax, Virginia. In the men's locker room, as we were dressing to play in the men's 70 event, one of the White players spoke to me and asked me if I remembered him. I did not, but then he helped me to recall our having played on several occasions on the red-clay courts in Ashbury, New Jersey, the summer of 1954.

First Time, ATA Circuit

I left Atlantic City by Greyhound bus in early July, going to Philadelphia, Pennsylvania. My plan was to play on the American Tennis Association (ATA) tournament circuit before reporting for military duty in El Paso, Texas, on September 28.

The ATA circuit was *the* thing for Colored players during this time of hard-core segregation, and many tennis families saved throughout the year, planning on "making the circuit." I had never played the circuit, which had a number of tournaments at that time, the first starting in Washington DC the weekend of July 4, hosted by the Mall Tennis Club. I had gone to the Nationals at Central State when I was a junior when some of the adults had sponsored me in the summer of 1948.

This was the second time I had seen so many good Negro players, men and women, and from that week on, I was determined to one day "play the circuit" on a regular basis. Years later, I would become president of the Mall Tennis Club. As I noted, I had played in the ATA National Championship as a junior in August of 1948 and again as an adult in Daytona Beach, Florida, in 1952. The next tournament on the circuit was in Baltimore, MD, played at Druid Hill Park, on the red-clay courts near the zoo; then, it was on to Philadelphia and the following week at Scotts Plains, New Jersey.

I got off the bus in Philadelphia around 5:00 pm on a Thursday evening at the tennis courts with my one bag and two tennis rackets.

Looking back, I am still awed that the Greyhound bus would take me to the tennis courts where the Colored played and not to the bus station!

There were several Colored men playing, and after I introduced myself, they welcomed me. When I told them I had won the National Intercollegiate Singles Championship in the past and had just graduated from Florida A&M, they were all very open to me. As it happened, one of the men playing was Junkie Woods, a disc jockey in Philadelphia. After we had stopped playing, someone asked me where was I staying, but I had no clue. Junkie invited me to stay with him and his wife. They had a very elegant house as I recall, and in the mornings, his wife took me to the courts. I stayed with them through Sunday morning.

The tournaments were usually Friday, Saturday, and Sunday, and at that time, I was good enough to win a few early rounds in the tournaments. I was given a ride by someone to Jersey for the next tournament, and I stayed with the Vaughns, Quent and Nana, in Newark. Nana, a left-hander, was one of the better female players. Up to this point, I had never seen very many good Colored female players. Some were very pretty, so this was quite a treat for this little southern boy!

This was the pattern "back in the day," because there were few Hotels that would accept Colored guests, and the concept of Motels was just nascent. More important, most players had very little money for hotels. Certainly I did not. After Jersey, the tournament moved to New York City, to Queens, where several red-clay courts were located behind the YMCA. A friend I met there was Bill Commack (now deceased), and we played doubles in the tournament. Bill had just started playing, and we lost in the first round.

I won a couple of early rounds in singles.

ATA Nationals

The big event was the ATA Nationals, held at Central State College, which was part of Wilber Force at that time, in Xenia, Ohio. George Stewart, from South Carolina State College and Panama, originally dominated the men's singles event but lost to Earthna Jacquet, a big serve and volley player from Los Angeles, California. Athena Gibson won the women's singles that year, beating Roumania Peters, "Big Pete," one of the Peters sisters. Little Pete, Margaret, was the other sister. Both are now deceased.

I did not play doubles, and I lost in an early round in the singles. I met some of the best Negro tennis players in the county during the summer of 1954, and over the next fifty years, I made many lifelong friends. The ATA circuit was to become very much a part of Jenk's and my lives; for me personally, I would meet Shirley Jones, my future wife and now wife of fifty-three years at one of the Nationals.

I would spend the next few weeks before reporting to the army in Washington DC with Mrs. Freeman, whom I had met earlier.

CHAPTER 5
THE MILITARY YEARS

September 28, 1954, I reported to Fort Bliss Army Base in El Paso, Texas, having taken a Greyhound bus in DC. I was twenty-one years old, and on my birthday, I would be twenty-two and a newly appointed Second Lieutenant and a US Army Artillery Officer. The first six weeks had to do with basic training, including classroom time on the weapons we would use (i.e., the thirty-five-millimeter antiaircraft guns and the M-16 rifle. The day began with physical exercise, starting at 0600 (6:00 am), Monday through Friday. We reported to the chow hall for breakfast at 0700 hour (7:00 a.m.), and classes started at 0800 hours!

About this time, I bought a used 1954 gray-and-black 88 Oldsmobile. Before I bought the car, I had taken my first driving test for a license in El Paso, and I failed the test. We were going down a one-way street, and I was driving in the middle lane and was told to make a left turn. We were about halfway down the block. I knew I should move to the curb lane before the turn, but I did not. Why? I don't know, and of course, I failed the test.

About a month later, I retook the test and passed. The next day, I bought my Oldsmobile 88 at a cost of about $1,000 and finished paying for it before I was discharged.

At that time, gas was twenty-one cents a gallon and postal stamps were three cents.

There was an important afternoon event in the city of El Paso, Texas, among the Negro society, and a prominent young Colored female needed an escort. For some reason, a Colored army officer was desired, and I was selected to be the escort. The evening consisted of dinner and dancing, and I escorted her back to her home.

Some years later, I would read that she had become very much involved as the bride of a very prominent politician in Ethiopia.

I attended Mass at a local Catholic Church in El Paso, where I met a very attractive young lady. Periodically, we went to a drive-in movie in the area, which was a favorite outing at that time.

I had the opportunity to play tennis on the base with several White players. In fact, we did have a tennis team and our coach was a White army Captain from Purdue University.

On the week-ends, many of us crossed the bridge and went over to Juarez, Mexico, to some of the clubs. One of our group, Chet, not Chet who played on the A&M tennis team, was arrested by the Mexican police on a Saturday night and kept overnight; however, he was released the following morning. We were never quite sure of the reason he was arrested, nor was he.

I had applied for Flight School, one of the options young Officers had for further training, although I knew full well Momma would not approve. Syl would have.

I was accepted, and some of my experiences are as recorded here.

Flight School

The army's Flight School was in San Marcos, Texas, 589 miles southeast from El Paso, Texas. We were trained in small fixed-winged planes, with one propeller, that were painted yellow. The plane was referred to as "the little yellow monster." I don't know the reason for the color except for clear identifications. Historically, "the area had terrain reportedly similar to that of Korea." This was during the time America was at war with Korea, and we were training to fly small fixed-winged planes over enemy lines and to get information for our antiaircraft artillery units for accurate firing on the enemy. Many of those who were lucky enough to complete flight training and fly over Korea during the war never made it back home alive.

Joe W., a classmate with whom I had become an Alpha at Florida A&M, a math major, and I were two of the five Negroes in the flight class.

There was a rumor well known by the Colored flight students that only one of the five would make the cut from each class.

One of the first barriers was the physical exam, especially the very critical eye exam. Several of us did not pass the exam, but the White eye Doctor did not seem too concerned. Since many of us had just arrived at San Marcos the day and evening before after a long drive, those of us who did not pass were told to get a good night's sleep, and we should be okay the next day when we were examined. He was correct because the next day everyone passed the eye exam and physical very easily. My initial problem had to do with completing all the paperwork. This was the first time I was confronted with the question of whom I was responsible to, even though I was twenty-two years old. Was it Syl, my biological mother, or Luella, whom I had called Momma from my earliest days?

Momma was absolutely against my flying, and I was very much concerned with disobeying her by entering Flight School. Syl, in contrast, had no problem with it. To this day, I believe my anxiety related to this dilemma was one of the reasons I never got the confidence I needed.

In the classroom, I had no problems, and in fact, I made the highest grades in the class on our first exam.

There was something about me making a very high grade on first exams.

For those who advanced in training by the sixth and seventh hour of actual flying, they were ready to move to the next level, to solo! I did not impress on my seventh hour, and I think the flight instructor sensed my insecurity. Initially, my first instructor was a young officer—all were White of course—and I felt relaxed with him. He would occasionally take us through some daredevil loops and spins. On the eighth hour, a different instructor was assigned to me, and I knew if I impressed him I could solo. I did not impress him, and I kind of knew it.

Within the next few days, I had to appear before a board of several White officers, and after a series of questions, they decided I did not qualify. There would be several more days before I would find out my new assignment. Of course, I was very disappointed and disheartened, but on some level, I think I tried to believe that nothing happens to us without The Lord allowing it.

There were interesting social events during my time at San Marcos.

Houston Tilliston College

When we left the base, we had the choice of turning left toward San Antonio, Texas, or right toward Austin, Texas. Most of the Colored officers turned right because that was the location of Houston Tilliston College, a Negro College. San Antonio and Austin were about equidistant from the base, about thirty miles. We had heard that a big dance was being held on one Friday evening at Houston Tilliston, so some of us put on our clean uniforms and our shiny gold second lieutenants' bars, and we went to the dance. Unlike my reluctance to socialize with the White girls at Texas Western in El Paso, I did meet a very attractive young lady early in the evening, and we spent most of the evening together talking and dancing.

What I did not know was that she apparently had a very jealous friend who objected to our spending all this time together. After getting her phone number and thinking about future dates, we parted around 10:30 or 11:00 p.m. when the dance was over.

When I went back to the car, all four of my tires had been cut! Someone was very upset, although I never found out who they were. Joe W., my classmate and frat brother, gave me a ride back to base, and the next day, Saturday, he gave me a ride back to the campus, and I was able to get the flats fixed without an incident.

Several week-ends later, some of us attended another dance at Houston Tilliston without any incidents. I did see the young lady I had previously met, but I did not spend all of the evening with her.

After the dance, for some reason, Joe W. and I decided to race back to the base at San Marcos.

I hit 100 miles per hour in my 88 Oldsmobile, and Joe passed me on the straight Highway 290.

The next morning, which was a Sunday, I went to Joe's room and saw that his car had been all but demolished. Somewhat aghast, I was greeted by Joe with "Hey, Tommy, how is it going?"

Joe was fine; the car was near totaled!

This was another occasion when I know our guardian angels were watching over us.

I completed the documents needed for transfer to my new location and waited for the phone call from headquarters. Joe did complete the training from our group, and years later, I read about him flying over to Cuba during Fidel Castro's regime. Some years later, FAMU had a reunion in DC, where I was a practicing General Surgeon. Joe, who was now an army Colonel, was there with his wife, and all in all, we had a great reunion.

Houston Tilliston is interesting itself in several respects. Dr. Herman A. Barnette III was a graduate and the first Negro student admitted to the University of Texas Medical School. Also, he was the first Negro to graduate and receive a license to practice medicine in the state of Texas.

Jackie Robinson (yes, of baseball fame) coached the school's men's baseball team in 1944–1945. Another major recognition for Houston Tilliston was that James A. Harris, a Scientist,(*) was part of the team that discovered and identified the Chemical Elements 104 and 105, part of the periodic table of chemical elements. Element 104 is rutherforidom (RF) an artificially produced radioactive element, and 105 dubnium (Db) is a synthetic radioactive element named after the town of Dubna in Russia. According to Wikipedia, the Soviet Joint Institute of Nuclear Research (JINR) reported the discovery in 1968. In 1970, the American Lawrence Berkeley Laboratory reported the discovery.

An official investigation by an international group of chemistry and physics decided the discovery should be shared by both Russia and America. In 1997, the element was officially named "dubnium" after the Russian town of Dubna, the site of the JINR.

(*) https://www.acs.org>acs>african-american-in-science.

The phone call came, and I went to the commanding officer to get my transfer orders. My orders were to report to the Thirty-Fifth Antiaircraft Artillery site at Fort Meade, Maryland. Part of the transfer included a two-week pass, of course all the while receiving my pay.

The dismissal from Flight School was bitterly disappointing and would take some time for me to get over, I thought. I enjoyed driving then, and the only handicap for us Negroes was there were no Hotels (Motels were not yet a generally accepted concept, as I previously noted) that accepted Negroes. Whenever fatigue set in, I would drive to a gas station, get gas, pull off at the edge of the station, crack the two back windows, and sleep, usually for a few hours.

A Herd of Horses

After Flight School, some of us were going back to Florida. I had my 1954 88 Oldsmobile, and we had heard there was going to be a party in Lake Charles, Louisiana, where one of the young ladies I had met at Houston Tilliston lived. She was having a party at her house. There were three of us, all Second Lieutenants, and we did make the party. I think we must have left her house sometime after midnight. I had the driving shift starting around 4:00 or 5:00 a.m., dawn, and as I recall, it was very foggy. At the party, I am sure all of us had been drinking, thankfully not too much. I remembered driving at a moderate speed because it was a foggy morning, and suddenly *a herd of horses* were coming at us in the middle of the highway! I swerved to the left to avoid them, and the car turned on its left side against a soft mud bank and stopped. Within seconds, the car righted itself, and the other guys, who were asleep, woke up, asking what had happened, apparently completely unaware!

I don't recall the conversation, but we continued on our journey with no further incidents, and I did not mention any details. I left the other guys on campus at FAMU and continued my drive to Jacksonville. Neither Momma nor Syl had seen me in my army uniform so that was a happy occasion for all.

During this time, Bill, my younger brother, who was still in High School at Stanton High, had to have his knee operated on and was in a full body cast for several months, which was the recommended treatment after surgery at that time. As he related to me recently and previously noted, he had been playing street football, as many of us did without our helmets or pads, and someone clipped him from behind, injuring his knee. He recalled that a lady friend of mine at that time, Carrie, and I came to visit him.

That had to have been a trying experience for him because he was left alone for most of the day while Syl worked unable to move. Syl always left food and water within reach, a Bible, reading material, and the phone. I visited several more times before I had to leave to report to duty at Fort Meade, Maryland. Later, Bill would graduate from FAMU in 1961with a Bachelor of Science in History and Political Science. After working for a year, he entered Epiphany College in New Burg, New York, the Josephite

Minor Novitiate for the Seminary of Saint Joseph, to study to become a Catholic Priest. Later he was moved to Saint Joseph Seminary in North East Washington, DC.

He indicates his desire to become a Priest was formed during the six months he had the plaster body cast, following Surgery for his broken leg.

He left the seminary after four years and got his Doctorate of Philosophy from Boston College in Psychology. He also told me that at a job interview, he met a young lady, Mary, who had been in the Convent preparing to become a Catholic Nun and had also left. He said she got the job, and they were later married. They have been now for fifty-four years. (Providence?)

They adopted a son, Billy, who was tragically killed in an automobile accident while attending Hampton University.

During the summer before reporting to Fort Bliss, at the tennis tournament in Queens, New York, I had met a young lady who lived in Corona, Queens. We had corresponded by letter periodically, and I called her using Syl's phone and told her I would be coming to New York. Syl thought I called Korea, but I reassured her it was only Queens, New York. I drove from Jacksonville to New York and arrived at her apartment near midnight on Sunday. Because of the lateness of the hour, I could only spend a short time visiting because I had to drive to Fort Meade, Maryland, about a three-hour drive, to report by 8:00 a.m.

Battery A, Baltimore, Maryland

After reporting to the commanding officer at Fort Meade, I was assigned to the Thirty-Fifth Antiaircraft Artillery (AAA) Company A (Ironically the same assignment I had in College in my ROTC unit and the same assignment I had during the summer ROTC training at Fort Bliss, Texas).

I cannot recall the name of the area, but it was quite a bucolic site, with the big antiaircraft artillery guns pointing over the Patapsco Bay.

We were at War with North Korea, and our primary responsibility was to protect the large steel mills on the Baltimore Harbor, steel of course being critical in the war effort. I can remember very clearly the day when I saluted and reported to the Captain of Battery A.

His words were "Got damn, Lieutenant, am I glad to see you!" This was a White Captain whom I would later learn drank heavily, and most of the running on base was done by the White Master Sergeant. The Captain left the base shortly after I reported, without any instructions or directions for me, and I never saw him again.

So, Second Lieutenant Calhoun was now the commanding officer of the Thirty-Fifth AAA Battery A, consisting of two Platoons, twelve men per Platoon, exactly as I had been trained in ROTC in College and ironically, my first assignment when I reported to Fort Bliss. Most of the soldiers were White men. There were only a few Colored soldiers. Their ranks were Privates, two Corporals (one in each Platoon), and a Master Sergeant. During that time, there was strict discipline and respect for the chain of command (i.e., respecting authority in the military).

The order of command, in ascending order, was private, corporal, sergeant, Master Sergeant, Second Lieutenant, First Lieutenant, Captain, Major, and various levels of Colonels and Generals. I was a Battery Commander, and at no time during my tour dates, all spent with Battery A, can I ever recall any disrespect to me as an officer because of my color.

There was an interesting event that occurred on the base.

There was a young White woman who accused one of the White soldiers of rape. As I was the Commanding Officer, I had to testify in the trial, the first time I would be involved with the legal system.

The incident was resolved as being consensual, both apparently having been heavily drinking.

I was not aware of any unusual activity occurring on the base at the time of the alleged event. I found out the next day the case was dropped.

On one occasion, the thought came to me to go to Wilmington, Delaware, to see if I could locate Bud. If one is a true believer, you know that things just don't happen by chance.

My Catholic faith helps me to believe this. I drove to Wilmington, less than two hours away from Baltimore on Highway 1 (Now Route 95 North) to an area where I saw some Colored men. One young man was coming out of an apartment building, and I asked him if he knew a Tom Calhoun.

To my surprise, he said yes and went back inside. Very shortly thereafter, Bud came out. I recognized him immediately.

I was in my army uniform, and the weather was warm and sunny. I shook his hand quite vigorously because I was truly glad to see him. About ten years had passed since I had seen him, so I may have introduced myself. I think I was about as tall as he was. He looked well. We stood and talked for quite a while.

At some point, I asked him if he ever thought about going back to Jacksonville to see Momma? He asked if I thought she would let him come back to the house, and I said, "Yes, I think she would."

I gave him twenty-five dollars and told him if he did go back, he had to stop drinking, which he promised he would do. I shook his hand again and left with a good feeling that I was able to see him.

On my drive back to Baltimore, I did say more than a few prayers of thanksgiving to the Good Lord for allowing me to contact him again.

After eighteen months, if officers performed well, we were automatically promoted to First Lieutenant and given two bright, shiny silver bars, and a pay raise. I was promoted to First Lieutenant and would ultimately be discharged as such when my two years were over. Soon after I was promoted, perhaps in a matter of months, a White First Lieutenant reported to Battery A. He was a few months senior to me, so I had to report to him.

At this time, there was a request from the Fort Meade base for those who would be interested in trying out for the base tennis team to report to Fort Meade. I had plans to report and try out for the team, but unfortunately, the new commanding officer did not allow me to do so, a very disappointing event, which in no way endeared me to him.

Over the eight or nine months of being stationed at Battery A, I would get a room at 35 Mulberry Street in Baltimore. One of the hall-marks of Baltimore at that time was the well-kept White "stoops" (steps) on many row houses, and 35 Mulberry Street had such steps.

I would meet a number of folk at Druid Hill Park on the asphalt tennis courts, as well as faculty and tennis players from Morgan State College. Also, there were several red-clay courts near the Zoo, but they were not used. I never knew the reason. Since I was one of the better tennis players in the area, I soon developed a number of friendly associates.

Some of my favorite memories were going to the well-known bars, the Comedy Club, and Club Tijuana, the Red Fox, and the Sphinx Clubs.

There were no charges to enter the Clubs, and costs for the drinks were very modest.

Near by the Sphinx Club was the Oblate Sisters Covent, the first Order of Black Nuns in America (obn), where Mother Elizabeth Lange who may soon become a Saint, was the Mother Superior.

(obn) https://www.blackpast.org>african-american-history>ob.

In 1955 and 1956, Billie Holliday, Carmen McRae, Charlie Parker, Oscar Peterson, Red Fox, and Ethel Ennis performed at the Red Fox Club in Baltimore. They were some of the entertainers I was able to see.

Operation Sagebrush

An interesting military event occurred before I finished my tour of duty. Operation Sagebrush consisted of several battalions of troops from Fort Meade, traveling overland to a small town in Louisiana. This happened during the time I was commanding officer of Battery A.

A large military truck pulled our artillery guns, and I enjoyed driving the truck some of those 1,222 miles. Our headquarters was established in the backyard of a White male landowner.

I suppose they were not a well-off family because the father offered his young teenage daughter to me to be paid for having sex with our troops.

I was shocked and surprised that a father would do that to his daughter but more surprised since he could see I was a Negro!

Needless to say, I told our troops that there would be *no* interaction with civilians!

The operation lasted a week, and while we did not fire any of our weapons, we did have many drills, day and night, simulating a wartime experience. Operation Sagebrush occurred toward the end of the second year of my army tour of duty.

A very hurtful event occurred about a week before my discharge. A White Lieutenant, a West Point graduate, and another White officer, whose name I cannot recall, called me. We had been on Operation Sagebrush together, and he asked if I would join him and the officer from West Point for some beers at the officer's club since we three were to be discharged the next day?

I agreed and felt very good that one of the White guys wanted me to be a part of their group, at least for that occasion. We met at the officer's club just outside of DC, talked, and had a few beers for several hours.

This was another active experience when Northern Racism was made very painfully clear to me. After the first beer, I was *completely* excluded from the conversation, and only rarely was there eye contact with me, and then mainly by the officer from West Point. I tried on multiple occasions to become involved in the conversation, but overall, I was pretty much excluded. When I finally realized what was going on, I wished both guys well and left.

In the many years since that occurred, there have been numerous occasions when I have been the only Black male in a discussion or social scenario with White men, and that same exclusion has occurred.

The country was still very much segregated in the period of 1954 through 1956, the time of my military tour of duty. The weekends when I was off duty I usually spent playing tennis during the days and at nights, "shaking the bushes, going to several nightclubs, fox hunting", as it was called, all in all, not very productive activities.

Through it all, I am very thankful that usually on Sunday mornings, I did get to Mass. I am sure there were many times I went to Confession, receiving the sacrament of Penance. At that time in the Catholic Church, one had to have abstained from food or drink at least twelve hours before receiving Communion. In the past few years, the requirement for fasting has become one hour before Mass. There were a number of Catholic Churches in Baltimore, but because of segregation, we Coloreds attended those only in certain parts of town.

Hernando's Hideaway

A vivid social event that occurred soon after I had transferred to Fort Meade comes to mind. In the military at that time, we got paid on the first of the month, so it was not surprising that on the first weekend after payday, when we were off duty, finding a party was the number-one priority. On one particular evening, a group of us officers visited a Club called Hernando's Hideaway. This was an off-limits Club and one of the few integrated spots in the Baltimore area. In 1956, as now, things did not really get rolling until around midnight!

There was only one entrance to the Club, which was downstairs. Around 12:00 or 12:30 a.m., the music was loud, and the drinks were flowing, when there were loud shouts from the top of the stairs, "THIS A RAID!"

Most of us, I'm sure, had A momentary weakness of our gastrointestinal tracts and our knees. Several White male police officers with weapons in hand came in, ordering everyone to move to one area of the club. My date, a Colored female, and I were near the entrance, and for some reason, we were allowed to leave.

To this day, I do not know why we were allowed to leave or what took place after we left, and we were not the only Negro couple present.

There were no integrated couples present.

The next day, there was a big article in one of the local newspapers—it may have been the *Baltimore Sun*—about a raid and arrest of several military officers at the illegal after-hours Hernando's Hideaway. I could not begin to imagine what would have happened if I were caught in such a raid.

I remember reading about it, and in hindsight, this was probably one occasion when I went to Confession, usually held on Saturday afternoons, and Mass the following Sunday morning.

Chemical Warfare Training

A more productive event during my army tour occurred at the Aberdeen, Maryland, US Army Base. I had planned to apply to medical school after the army. I had the foresight at that time, that even if I was accepted to a medical school, I was not emotionally prepared for the academic rigors and regimentation. Somehow, I felt pretty sure I would be accepted at some medical school, and I would find the financial resources needed.

Howard University in Washington DC and Meharry Medical College in Nashville, Tennessee, were the only two places where Negro men could go to medical school as far as I knew.

At that time, very few females of any race attended medical schools.

It happened that there was an occasion when I was in DC, and the idea came to me to visit the medical school at Howard. I recall going to the Dean's office to express my interest in medicine, and it happened that I was able to speak directly with the Dean. I remember him as a very light-skinned man, very elegant and professional in appearance. We spoke at the door of his office, as I was not invited in, and I'm sure he discouraged me from applying to Howard. At the time, I did not know why. Of course, I was very disappointed but not discouraged.

Later, I would find out that brown- or dark-skinned individuals were not desired at Howard.

This was my second encounter with bigotry from another Colored person. The first such incident had occurred on an earlier visit to DC.

The Alphas had a fraternity house in DC, and I went for a visit, introducing myself as a brother from the Beta Nu chapter of FAMU in Tallahassee, Florida. I expected a friendly, cordial visit because that was what we did when visited by other brothers at FAMU. It took me a few minutes before I perceived that I was not welcome … and I deduced it was because of my color. The brother whom I met was very fair!

A few weeks before I would be discharged from the army, I had the opportunity to get some additional training, which many years later, would be very helpful for me in my work career. I had noted a request in some of the many memos that came across my desk from headquarters at Fort Meade. One memo asked for individuals who had an interest in chemical warfare to report to Aberdeen, Maryland, about thirty-five miles from my base outside of Baltimore, about an hour's drive. I would spend a week there with academic classes on various chemicals, such as mustard gas, chlorine, and hydrogen cyanide to mention a few. Classes were from 0800 to 1600 hours (8:00 a.m. to 4:00 p.m.) Monday through Friday with a final written exam on Friday morning and a field exercise in the afternoon. Classroom studying included proper understanding of and use of various gas masks, personal protection equipment (PPE), and decontamination procedures, as well as learning the actions and effects of various chemical agents. The final field exercise exam required our group to be in full military gear, which included our M-16 rifles without live ammunition, a water canteen, and a standard M Series Gas Mask as part of our PPE.

We were taken to a dimly lit, closed room with no windows.

Prior training consisted of numerous drills on holding our breath for at least thirty seconds and safely putting on our Gas Masks in ten seconds! Drills would occur unannounced throughout the day, whether in the classroom or outside with a training officer shouting, "GAS, GAS"!

Once we were in the room, about twelve by twelve feet, with the door securely closed, a container was thrown into the room and exploded, emitting a yellowish gas. We heard somebody shout, "GAS, GAS"!

I am sure we were all pretty scared, but most of us did get our Gas Masks on properly in the ten seconds or less. A few men were unsuccessful and began to yell and scream. When the door was opened and we all exited the room to fresh air, we would find out that the agent was tear gas or (CN phenyl chloride), also now popularly known as "Mace." Within a few minutes of being outside, the men who had been crying had recovered with no lasting eye damage but with busted egos.

The obvious lesson loud and clear was if this had been a fatal gas agent or if one were in a confined area without a mask or the knowledge of how to use one properly, serious illness or death could have occurred.

Honorable Military Discharge

I left Fort Meade, just outside of Baltimore, Maryland, on Friday, September 27, 1956, around 1400 hours (2:00 p.m.). Historically, September 28, 1956, was the last night of the Johnny Carson TV show and the birthday of Boris Yeltzin, former Russian president.

Ed Geiger, the brother of David Geiger of whom I spoke earlier, and Eddie Major, also from Jacksonville, Florida, were discharged that same day. Eddie Major would become a Lawyer and practiced in Los Angeles, California, for some time. I heard he expired about ten years ago. I never had any follow-up information on Ed Geiger. The distance from Baltimore to Nashville is approximately 700 miles. In 1956, there were only two-lane highways and the speed limits were somewhere between fifty-five and sixty-five miles per hour, depending on the state in which you were driving. For the most part, states determined speed limits within their boundaries.

As I have previously noted, I know that my guardian angel has been watching over me. I had planned to drive all night and arrive in Nashville,

Tennessee, Saturday morning. Sometime during the early morning, I was driving toward Knoxville, Tennessee, approximately 180 miles from Nashville. Even now, I remember it was a very foggy morning on Highway 40 West, which I had taken leaving Baltimore, and it was very hilly. I could not see the signs clearly, and I remember stopping and getting out of the car to get a closer look at the directions. When I looked out from in front of my car, my 1954 Oldsmobile, I was looking down a jagged, rocky crevice, into which I may well have driven or fallen had I not stopped! I backed up and slowly found my way back to the main highway.

I probably did not thank my guardian angel as I should have!

CHAPTER 6
NASHVILLE, TENNESSEE

I arrived in Nashville, Tennessee, early Saturday morning, September 28, 1956. I was not sure where I would live, but that had never been an impediment for me in the past. I did get a room that day with three Meharry medical students, in their third year.

There was small Club on Jefferson Street which some one pointed out, and I went in, and joined some guys drinking beer. I met J.R., O.C., and "Little John", who lived in a house on Jefferson Street, near-by, each with his own room, and there was an unoccupied room, which they rented to me. J.B. would graduate the following year and after a residency in ophthalmology would begin his practice in Detroit, Michigan. Little John, became a psychiatrist and also practiced in Detroit. OC completed his residency in Obstetrics and Gynecology, but I'm not sure where he set up his practice.

The reason I went to Nashville was to increase my chances for entering Meharry Medical College.

If one googles Meharry Medical College, one will find a summary of its history described in "The Salt Wagon Story … an Act of Kind Men".

"In the 1880s, sixteen year old White Samuel Meharry was hauling a load of salt through Kentucky when his wagon slid off the road into a muddy ditch. With darkness approaching and a cold wintry rain, he searched for help. He saw a cabin, the home of a freed Negro slave family he would discover. Although the family was still vulnerable to slave bounty hunters, they risked their freedom and gave Samuel food and shelter for the night.

Came morning light, they helped lift his wagon from the muddy ditch and Meharry continued on his journey. Very touched by the family's kindness, he is reported to have said, {I have no money now, as he departed, but when I am able, I will do something for your race]".

There is no record of the Negro family.

Samuel Meharry would grow prosperous over the ensuing years. Some forty years later, as the Civil War ended, a group of leading White Methodist clergymen and laymen organized the Freedom Aid Society in August 1866 to "elevate former slaves, intellectually and morally." Getting Negroes involved in this movement, Samuel Meharry and his four brothers acted, pledging their support to Central Tennessee College, an emerging medical education program with $30,000 in cash and real properties, repaying the Negro family's kindness.

In 1876, they founded the College's medical department, which over time became known as Meharry Medical College.

Fisk University

When I arrived in Nashville, classes had already begun at Fisk University. Since I had a bachelor of science degree from FAMU in premed, heavily weighted in biology, I had some discussions about work in the Department of Biology, but there was none. I was told that perhaps I could connect with the Department of Chemistry. I met with the Chair, Dr. Samuel Massie, now deceased, and he accepted me into the graduate program to work toward a master's degree in chemistry, also providing a partial work scholarship.

Fisk is literally across the street from Meharry, and the house in which I would be living on Jefferson Street was less than ten minutes' walking distance.

My performance in Chemistry, during my first weeks of the semester, was disastrous. I had poor study habits, and with all those "pretty young thangs"—girls—at Fisk and Tennessee State University ten minutes from where I lived, my social and party demons were still very much extant.

Much of the first semester was not very productive academically, and I am sure Dr. Massie must have questioned his decision to accept me into the program. As I reflect on those times, I find it really embarrassing because I could not answer any of my oral questions. To be fair, I did not have a strong Chemistry base on which I could rely, as I was a Premed major in college, with classes heavily weighted toward Biology.

I began feeling sorry for myself after a while because I knew my performance was not reflective of who I was.

There was a redeeming performance, however, when I was given an assignment to present to the class a discussion on acetyl salicylic acid—aspirin. The blackboard and chalk were the primary visual tools at that time; slides and PowerPoint were not yet nascent. A technique I had learned in the army was to use a lead pencil and write key parts of your discussion on the blackboard. The audience could not see what was written, only the presenter. I came in early and wrote the formulae and key bits of information on the blackboard. I really prepared for the presentation. By then, my pride was hurt because I knew I could do better.

My presentation was outstanding! I was able to write my formulae during the presentation while referring to my pencil-written notes. Was this cheating? No, because slides and PowerPoint presentations visually point out this information, and my overall class grade for that first semester was a "B."

I had made other contacts in the Biology department and second semester since I did have a bachelor's degree (BS) in Premed and my grades were pretty good in College, I was given the position of Instructor, teaching Botany, Biology, and Parasitology, and also helping out in the lab. I withdrew from the Chemistry program. In the lab, my job was to feed white mice a special liquid mixture by using a small glass tube and inserting it into esophagus of the mouse and keeping the mice cages clean.

Years later, after I had completed medical school and a residency in General Surgery, I met Dr. Massie at several social events in DC, and we had pleasant conversations.

There were several very smart and pretty young ladies in my classes at Fisk. One was a very bright young lady who averaged ninety-seven on all of her exams. She wanted to become a Doctor. Since I was hoping to go to medical school also, I followed her pursuit. She applied to medical school at the University of Florida but was not accepted.

She was very disappointed and distraught, but segregation was still very much the law of the land, so it was not surprising she was not accepted.

I don't remember if she had applied to other medical schools.

I continued teaching at Fisk through June 1957, interspersed with parties and tennis … and of course going to Sunday Mass.

When I first arrived at Fisk, I was able to play tennis with some of the guys on the team, two of whom I knew from playing in Cleveland, but as the school year progressed, their schedules did not allow for much play.

I did play the ATA Nationals at Central State in August 1957. I did not have much money although I had been teaching at Fisk, so I pawned my one good tailor-made suit for ten dollars, and I got a ride from Nashville with some folk who were going to Dayton, Ohio, and to the Central State College campus. I would get a ride back to Nashville, but I cannot remember with whom.

I remember losing to Leon Bowser from Baltimore, Maryland, 4-6,4-6. I regularly beat him when I was in the army and living in Baltimore. Also, one reason the occasion is so vivid is that he also won a car that was being raffled off at the Nationals that year.

Jenk and I would lose to him and Walter Moore at the 100th Anniversary of the ATA Nationals in the finals of the Men's 80 Doubles, 5-7,0-6, on Thursday, August 4, 2017, in Baltimore, Maryland, where the first Nationals were played in 1917.

This would be the last time Jenk and I played tennis together.

Jenk and I had been corresponding periodically by mail, and he came to Nashville in September or October of 1957.

The Reunion

In either September or October of 1957, Jenk came to Nashville and he was able to bunk with me at the house on Jefferson Street. This was great because we started playing tennis almost daily, planning on making the ATA circuit that summer. Further, Jenk was a good influence on me because I stopped much of the partying and started training for the circuit.

He was able to get work at the post office, and I was still teaching at Fisk.

During that time and even now, most US Post Offices throughout the country were very busy for the two weeks during the Christmas holidays, so I was able to pick up some much-needed cash by working there also.

Two potentially life-changing incidents occurred during this time in Nashville.

The first incident occurred one winter afternoon as I was leaving the movies and walking back to where I lived, and a White motorcycle-riding policeman stopped me and asked where I had been. I was wearing a tan winter trench coat, and I had a cap on. I told him I was just leaving the movies and showed him the ticket stub, which I had in my pocket.

He told me, "You better go take off that coat because you fit the description of a guy who just robbed a jewelry store downtown." I am sure I said some thank you prayers after that.

There were two times I can recall when I locked my car keys in the car.

The first was during the Christmas holidays of 1956 when I worked at the post office to get some extra cash.

I had to break the window on the driver's side to get into the car. About the same time, a White lady asked me to look under her car, which was parked nearby because she thought something had broken. I had crawled under the car and found nothing, and as I was getting on my feet to tell her, there was a White guy with an iron pipe drawn back to hit me. I told him I was trying to help the lady, who quickly agreed, averting another potentially life-altering incident.

The second locked key incident occurred here in DC several years ago. I had taken Shirley to the National Rehab Center for an appointment and parked in the front driveway as I retrieved her wheelchair from the trunk, a two to three-minute action I thought. When I went back to open the door to get into the car … whoops, the key was locked in. I asked a police officer at the desk if she had an instrument or coat hanger I could use to get the key, and she said no.

I was in a mini panic mode now because I was blocking the entry to a very busy rehab facility, and I needed to move my car. My thought was to call AAA, but that was going to take some time.

Again, my guardian angel came to the rescue! I had left the window on the passenger side partially open. A young man with cleaning material was entering the building, and I asked him if he knew where I could get a coat hanger. He said no, but when I told him the problem, he was able to reach in through the open window and unlock the door. Fortunately, he was slight of stature and easily unlocked the door. Yes, I know he was my guardian angel at that time.

Hadley Park, about ten minutes from Tennessee State University, is where Jenk and I practiced almost daily. The tennis courts were Har-Tru, the surface referred to as clay throughout the country. (Har-Tru, commonly referred to as clay, is a natural green stone made from metabasalt, found in the Blue Ridge Mountains of West Virginia.)[3] There is some controversy as to whom the park was named after. Some historians claim it was named after John Hadley, a White slave owner, while others claim it was named after Dr. W. Hadley, an African American physician, a graduate of Meharry Medical College, a few blocks from the park.

In August of 1955, Jenk and I played our first ATA Nationals at Central State, and we lost to the Freeman brothers, Clyde and Harold, from Washington DC, the number-one-seeded team in the first round.

Jenk had been recently honorably discharged from the Air Force, and I was on leave from the army so we did not have much practice time together. We had won the toss and elected to serve first. In the past, I always started serving, and that had been a good strategy for us, as we had never lost that first game. After the initial five-minute warm-up, I reached up to hit a forceful first serve and felt a sudden, sharp, agonizing pain in my lower stomach! At this time, I was not that familiar with human anatomy. We finished the match, losing in two sets. I could not raise my right arm above my shoulder without severe pain. After the match, I went behind a nearby building and cried unashamedly. Looking back now as a General Surgeon, I know I sustained a partial tear of my right rectus abdominus muscle. There is a left muscle also.[4]

These two muscles make up the so-called *six-pack* of muscles that run down the front of the abdomen.

Strenuous sexual activity by the male can result in this type of injury also.

In August 1958, after the ATA Nationals, Jenk, Sara Allen, her daughter Leslie Allen (about whom more will be said later), and I left

---

[3] hartru.com>pages>har-tru--green.

[4] *Gray's Anatomy*, 35th edition (WB Saunders Co., 1973), 523–524.

Xenia, Ohio, and arrived at 3005 Eleventh St. NW, in DC, to stay with Mrs. Freeman. Sarah had a Blue Nash, and the front seats would collapse backward, which made it much easier to sleep in. We had been invited by Mrs. Freeman, with whom we had reconnected at the Nationals, to stay with her before we left.

The Nationals represented the end of the year for organized tennis for us Colored players.

Jenk and I had started the ATA tennis circuit in Washington DC, playing in the Mall Tennis Club's event, one of the premier circuit events, if not *the* premier event, we would later learn.

It would be at this event where Jenk and I won our first men's double championships and Jenk the men's singles title. We would become a force to be reckoned with. Beginning the weekend of July 4, the circuit moved to Baltimore, Philadelphia, New Jersey, and Queens, New York. At each of these tournaments, Jenk and I were invited to stay with a tennis family.

In New York, Jenk and I stayed with Jenny and Jim Glass, both now deceased. They had two sons, one of whom, Louis, played on the tennis team at the University of California at Los Angeles (UCLA), where Arthur Ashe had played. Indeed, most of the out-of-town players were invited to stay with local families, the host club having made these arrangements prior to the tournaments starting. This was necessary because most motels and hotels were not open to Negroes, and many of us did not have the financial means to pay for these services even if they were open to us.

Jenk won most all the singles events except in Baltimore, where he lost in the finals to Buzzy Hettleman, who was about five feet five inches in height but was able to run down and return most of the balls Jenk hit.

At the Nationals this year, 1962, in the doubles semifinals, Jenk and I had our first experience with Negro politics in tennis.

I had heard a rumor that the New York crowd for some reason did not like Jenk, something he and I had not talked about. I believe it was because he was winning most of the tournaments, having beaten some of the New York players in prior tournaments, especially George Stewart, who had not lost a singles match until Jenk beat him.

According to the rules, players had to be *on* the courts fifteen minutes before the match start time. (Actually, the rule indicated that a player must be at the court no later than fifteen minutes of the start time or the match was subject to default.)

Jenk and I were walking to the gate for our semifinals match when Mr. Spooner, the Umpire, now deceased,, shouted out to us, "You are defaulted!"

I asked, quite irritated, "Why?"

He said, "You were not *on* the courts."

Jenk and I went to the officials' office to present our case but were told it was the Umpire's decision. Jenk was scheduled to play the finals in singles, and he told me he was not going to play. We discussed the situation at length, and I am sure I convinced him that he should play, which he did. I do not know if that event was a factor, but he lost to Billy Davis in spite of having three match points! At the Nationals the next year, August 1958, we won the men's doubles title, and the team of Jenkins and Calhoun was established as the best Negro men's doubles tennis team in the country.

We would reach the finals during many of the ensuing years, winning the title on two occasions, the last in 1960.

We played in the doubles National finals at Hampton, Virginia, in August 1961, losing to Arthur Ashe and Ronald Charity in five sets.

Arthur easily won the singles, beating Jenk in three straight sets. We reached the finals again in 1962, losing to Billy Davis, and his brother Bobby.

The culmination of the tennis summer circuit was the nationals held at Central State College in Xenia, Ohio. Central State had been a part of Wilber Force University. According to Wikipedia, in 1941, the National and Industrial Departments split from Wilber Force and were renamed Central State College and later, in 1965, Central State University.

The Nationals, by many Negro standards, was one of the foremost social and athletic events of the year in the Negro society. The College opened the dormitories for a nominal daily charge, and the cafeteria was opened for breakfast, lunch, and dinner, also at nominal charges.

During the summer, most College dormitories were closed, so this was a money-making event for the school. Because Jenk and I had won most of the doubles events along the circuit and Jenk had won many of the singles' titles, the ATA board gave us free room and board … free breakfast, lunch, and dinner, treats which we had no idea we would receive when we began the event.

We were traveling to all of the events in my 1954 Oldsmobile, which was now slowly succumbing to wear and tear.

At each of these tournaments, Jenk and I were invited to stay with a tennis family.

CHAPTER 7
MADISON, KENTUCKY

Jenk and I were traveling to all of the events in my Oldsmobile 88, which was now slowly succumbing to wear and tear. I recalled when we left Nashville, Tennessee, in late May of 1958, heading to St. Louis, Missouri, for a tournament we had entered at the outskirts of Madison, Kentucky, the motor began to smoke. Jenk and I by no means were or are saints, but the Good Lord watches over sinners and saints alike. Madison is a small town in east central Kentucky, the site of Berea College in 1855.

According to the Madison County Historical Society, the Berea Mission School (bms) was established "to educate blacks and whites together on a basis of equality, making it one of the first interracial schools in the United States."

"The school came about as a result of efforts by the Reverend Gregg Fee and Cassius Marcellus Clay" (the ancestor of Cassius Clay or Muhammad Ali).

(bms) https://www.madisoncountykyhistory.org>history>co.

It was about 11:00 or 11:30 a.m. on a Saturday morning when the Oldsmobile sort of gave out. There was an auto repair shop on our left as we were driving through on I-75. This was the segregated South so it was with a bit of trepidation that we drove to the shop. We asked if they could repair the car and also boldly asked if they knew if there were any Colored families we could stay with. They would not be able to get the car repaired before Monday.

So The Good Lord knew our situation, and the White men took us to the home of a Colored family, no more than two blocks from the repair shop and within a hundred yards or less of two tennis courts with cement surfaces. Jenk and I were welcomed into the family's home; I do not remember their names. We were fed very well, and we asked the wife about the tennis courts. She said they were for Whites only, but Jenk and I practiced about an hour and a half with no one telling us to leave. No White players showed up to play. We practiced the next day, Sunday, also without difficulty. We were treated to Sunday meals, and at no time were we asked for money, although I am sure Jenk and I sincerely offered to pay for something.

About midday on Monday, the men from the repair shop came and told us the car had been repaired. I don't know what we paid them. At that time, I am sure Jenk and I did not see or think much about the Lord's hand in this activity. As I write this, I am sincerely thankful to the Good Lord for this and all the many, many blessings we received throughout our lives.

Saint Louis Country Club

We would drive on to St. Louis and were allowed to play in the tournament at the Saint Louis Country Club. As Jenk and I went out to play, we could see Colored faces looking out from windows and doors and would later understand this was the first such occasion when Coloreds were allowed to play tennis at the Club.

I remember we wanted Cheeseburgers and French fries for lunch, and this was our first time of learning that one does not pay for food or drinks at the Club. When one is sponsored by one of the members, there is no charge. One of the Club members who had seen us play did sponsor our meal.

We had no way of knowing that our first round opponent was either the number-one or two seed in the tournament. We had to play the number-one-seeded doubles team, a father and son, and they beat us rather easily. To be sure, we were affected by knowing that we were the only Coloreds in the tournament and quite honestly were overawed by the occasion!

We both lost our singles matched also, to top-seeded players.

This would be the pattern we Negro players would experience for years to come when we entered Open tournaments (i.e., that those in which our entries were accepted).

Sadly, I noted this same practice some thirty years later; the Black players usually had to play a higher seed in the early rounds, and the same when our children would enter many of the local and out-of-state tournaments.

The Pink Suitcase

I remember Jenk and I had just arrived at the Nationals and were sitting beside the courts when Althea Gibson and Karol Fageros, now deceased, joined us. Althea and I recognized each other from our days as students at FAMU. She and Jenk also recognized each other. I had practiced with her a few times at FAMU. I never won more than two to three games in a set. Karol Fageros (cf) was this very beautiful blond female who had teamed with Althea in Miami, Florida, in what was a nascent attempt to start a female professional tennis circuit. They did not play in the ATA Nationals, and we did not see them anymore that week.

According to the New York Times "Karol Fageros, in 1958, after she wore gold lame underpants in the French Open, Wimbledon officials banned her. She was reinstated the next year. She died at age 53 from Cancer in 1988".

(cf) nytimes.com/1988/04/14/obituaries/karol-fageros-short-tennis-champion-53.html.

Wednesdays were always the deciding days at the Nationals. This was because with play starting on Mondays, by the end of play on Wednesday afternoon, only the good players were left. The quarterfinals were played Thursdays, then semifinals on Fridays, and the finals that Saturday, unless there had been a rain date; then the finals were on Sundays. I remember later on Wednesday afternoon looking on court 6, when the last match of the day was being played between Shirley Jones and Carolyn Williams. During the early part of the week, I had started a conversation with Shirley, whom I really wanted to get to know better.

As one can imagine, by Wednesday afternoon, after we had played and practiced early in the week, our tennis outfits, including towels and socks, were in need of a laundry fix. Jenk was not the aggressor in taking care of laundry; I was. I am sure this was in part due to my training as an officer in the army, where we had five-day-a-week inspections of our rooms, clothing, and shoes. I usually collected our well-worn tennis shorts, shirts, towels, and socks and put them in a pillowcase. We each had at least two pairs of "jock straps," which we had to keep clean as best we could, remembering that we were playing when the daily temperatures were in the low to high 90 degrees Fahrenheit. Jenk and I did not have many outfits, probably three pairs of shorts and shirts, and I am thinking at least five or six pairs of white socks and probably a couple of towels each.

At this time in tennis culture, the outfits had to be completely white, so in order to keep ours white, I used a lot of bleach when washing our things. Over time, the pillowcase in which I had our things for washing had become pink as things faded from the bleach. Lucy and Shirley had an iron in their room, and Jenk and I did not, so on this particular day, I asked Lucy if they would iron our shorts from our *"pink suitcase,"* or if I could use their iron.

I am sure during this time I began to have serious feelings for Shirley.

The previous Saturday afternoon, Shirley and I and several other Catholics went to the afternoon Mass, which counted for Sunday Mass in Xenia. After Mass, a group of us went to the movies to see the new movie just coming out, *From Russia with Love*, the first of many 007, James Bond, movies, starring Sean Connery and Ursula Andress.

Shirley was teaching high school in Cleveland, and after the Nationals, she returned to Cleveland. Jenk and I also went to Cleveland because we had told Sarah Allen, now deceased, whom we had met earlier, that we would help her move to DC with her daughter Leslie.

We stayed overnight with Sarah, and Shirley and I spent time together talking and getting to know each other better.

My car was worn out by this time, and since Jenk and I had no financial means for repairs, I left my Oldsmobile 88 on the Street in Cleveland.

Jenk and I left for DC the next day with Sarah and Leslie in her Blue Nash. All of us were able to stay with Mrs. Freemen, with whom we had reconnected at the Nationals.

CHAPTER 8

MEHARRY MEDICAL COLLEGE

I returned to Nashville, Tennessee, in September of 1959 to begin my freshman year as a medical student at Meharry Medical College, at age twenty-seven. The ten months I had worked at the US Post Office in DC had prepared me mentally for the regimentation and routine I thought would be needed to succeed at Meharry.

Just as important, I had made a nice bit of money, much of which I saved because I had to pay Mrs. Freeman, with whom I was staying, only a few dollars.

Mrs. Lucille Freeman (now deceased), the mother of Dr. Clyde Freeman, Tommy (now deceased) and Dr. Harold Freeman, now living in New York City, should be called "the Godmother of Black tennis" because of the kindness she showed to many of us young players who stayed at her house at 3005 Eleventh Street, NW, in DC.

While living at 3005, I attended regular Sunday 9:00 am Mass at Sacred Heart Catholic Church, located on Park Road and Sixteenth Street NW. After Mass, I would often stop at a Waffle and Egg Café on Park Road for waffles, eggs, sausage, and milk, all for about two dollars. After my last Mass at Sacred Heart, I went to the front of the Church, where a large statue of the crucified Christ was located on the right, my left as I looked toward the altar. I knelt before the statue and prayed with both hands on the nailed feet of Jesus, begging Him to help me use my hands, my life, to help my fellowman as a Physician, a Surgeon, which was my wish. I was motivated to succeed in part because Harold Freeman, one of Mrs. Freeman's sons with whom Jenk and I stayed at 3005, had been accepted into medical school at Howard University in DC and was training to become a Surgeon.

My personal belongings consisted of two suits (one blue serge), two pairs of shoes plus my tennis shoes, two racquets, shirts and underwear, several pair of pants, my army clothes and toiletries, all in my green army duffel bag.

The past two summers, tennis-wise, Jenk had won most of the singles matches, and he and I won most of the doubles match we played, for which were given large trophies. We left those trophies at Mrs. Freeman's house.

Along with my letter of acceptance to Meharry was information regarding my living quarters, a two-story men's dormitory on campus.

Interestingly, the day after I received my letter of acceptance to Meharry, I also received an acceptance letter from Howard!

My roommate, Larry Young, from Hampton, now deceased, and I had the end room on the second floor of the men's dormitory.

Larry's bed was near the window, mine was near the door, and our desk was in about the center of the room.

There was a central bathroom, midway on the second floor, with two sinks, a washbasin, and four showers.

The Good Lord always has a plan for us. If He did not, we would be in a heap of trouble. I did have some money from my job at the post office, as Mrs. Freeman had not charged Jenk and me or Sarah and her daughter Leslie any rent. We did give her some money when we had some. I knew that my GI Bill (Government Issue, the Serviceman's Readjustment Act of 1944) would start in October, so I would have some additional cash coming in.

This act was initially signed into law by President Franklin D. Roosevelt, originally for White men only; however, it became available to Colored ex-military men 1959.

On my first day, I did apply for financial aid from the administrator at Meharry and was fortunate (blessed) in being granted a $250 award, which went directly to the school.

One of the first people I met on my first day at Meharry was Earl Thomas Cullins, one of the original Black Hawks from Jacksonville. Earl had graduated from Stanton High School in Jacksonville in January 1949, and as I have previously noted, he went off to Kentucky State College and then the army. This was September 1959, meaning it had been ten years since I last saw Earl, who was now starting his senior year in medical school. Earl was also a member of the Alpha Phi Alpha Fraternity. (Note comments about him in the introduction.)

I said the Lord has His plans, and our meeting, in my mind, was surely by His design. Earl gave me his microscope, which all freshmen and sophomores needed, without charge. He also encouraged me and helped prepare me for some of the pitfalls that would arise throughout the ensuing years. I also met Ray Cutts (now deceased), also a senior, who was one of my senior fraternity brothers at FAMU and initiated me into the fraternity. Ray also gave me some pointers on how to get through the years at Meharry.

After I got my living quarters arranged, I next found the nearest Catholic church to Meharry. Although I cannot recall the name of the church, it was about ten minutes' walking distance from my living quarters, and I was a frequent visitor the next four years. The first two years at Meharry were primarily concerned with reading, memorizing, and praying on my part. The average twenty-four-hour day included perhaps four to five hours of sleep.

The first semester was traumatic, and one of the reasons had to do with the welcoming dinner for the freshmen.

We met all of our instructors, and ironically and surprisingly, many of them greeted us with the air of "I got mine, good luck to you!"

I believe the level of maturity each student had, played a major role in how we interpreted that statement.

To summarize the feelings of many of us who would graduate in four years (some would not but did have the opportunity to repeat the year if they failed, and in fact, there were two of our classmates who were repeating), avowed they would never give back to Meharry because of the way they felt we were treated.

Another reason was the system of *redlining* the names of those who failed Physiology, posting the names on the Bulletin Board outside the classroom.

The course was taught by a husband and wife team.

I stayed in Nashville over the Christmas holidays, and I remember working for them, cleaning their house and performing other handyman activities. I had made good grades on the exams and I am sure my demeanor was pleasing to them.

Redlining, the same punishment for freshmen who failed the first year at FAMU, as I previously noted, seemed cruel and unnecessary to many of us.

Bombing

WCKY was a Radio Station that broadcast out of Cincinnati, Ohio. The reception was great around 2:00 or 3:00 am when many of us were studying.

A major social event happened our freshman year. The station reported an uprising of College students at West Virginia State in Institute, West Virginia, in a movement toward integration. The movement had been gradually gaining momentum on predominantly Black College campuses.

During that time, there was a Negro Lawyer in Nashville who had gained some notoriety through high-profile cases he was involved with. I cannot remember his name.

For a while, there had been numerous organized *sit-ins*, usually involving predominately Negro College students. These *sit-ins* consisted of a group of College students and their supporters, some White, who would enter a well-known White establishment that served Whites only and *sit-in* at the counters, asking to be served. They were all nonviolent sit-ins, and usually the White police would show up and force them to leave. If there was resistance, they would be arrested.

Most weekdays, I was up at 5:00 am studying, often preparing to go to 6:30 am Mass.

On this particular morning, I had just finished shaving and dressing when a loud explosion occurred across the street from our dorm.

From my military experience, I knew immediately it was a bomb!

The force shattered the windows in our dorm room. Larry, my roommate, was still in bed near the window and sustained multiple facial cuts from the blast, none of which were serious. I walked to the end of the hallway, and looking out the window, I saw the entire back room of the house across the street had been blown away. This was the home of the Negro lawyer and his wife.

As humans, we often need to be reminded that The Lord is in charge (He has the whole world in His hands), and nothing happens unless He allows it.

Soon after the explosion, as daylight was beginning, the Lawyer and his wife came outside from the front part of the house, which had not been damaged by the blast.

In my mind, the Good Lord had orchestrated their sleeping arrangement that night.

As daylight and morning were full upon us, the entire Meharry Medical College Community was now awake. Fisk University, which was across the street on the east side, had come to life, as had the entire surrounding neighborhood. Tennessee State University, less than a mile away, likewise was well aware of the incident.

Thinking about the idea of unintended consequences, instead of the bomb harming or killing a civil rights leader, as the Lawyer was rapidly evolving toward, the Negro community became alive, galvanized, and organized. Classes were stopped at Meharry, Fisk, and Tennessee State University.

By midday, an organized march of students and staff from each of the schools to downtown Nashville before the City Official's offices was underway.

Over the ensuing days, classes would resume at the three colleges, but the movement was well underway. In February 1960, multiple *sit-ins* at counters at White establishments took place all over the South.

Not surprisingly, legal action was never taken against whoever was responsible for the bombing. Nashville became the center of organized *sit-ins* during the early part of the movement.

I finished the first year of Meharry in good standing and came back to DC the summer of 1960, again staying in the basement of 3005 Eleventh Street NW, with Mrs. Freeman. Clyde, her eldest son, and I got jobs for the first part of summer with the DC Recreation Department.

In the afternoons, after work, we played tennis.

In August of 1960, Jenk and I won our second national doubles title, the first in 1959, at Central State in Ohio.

Jenk had left DC to start school in St. Louis, Missouri, at St. Louis University on a tennis scholarship and the GI Bill in 1959.

I started my sophomore medical school year in September in good standing. The first part of the year was still classroom study, and two of the major classes were Pathology and Pharmacology. I was able to go back home to Jacksonville, Florida, for the two weeks of Christmas break. Most of my time was spent studying Pathology because we were told there would be a major Pathology exam when we returned from the Christmas holidays.

My brother, Bill, was in College now at FAMU, having entered as a freshman in 1956.

Bud, Tom Calhoun, after whom I was named had returned to Jacksonville, and he and Momma had a few years together before he died. I remember she told me that on one occasion, he had passed a "lot of s**t, black as tar" before he died. *Colon cancer?* I wondered.

I often wonder what kind of life the two of them had when he returned. She said he had stopped drinking.

The two-week break was all too short, and we returned to Meharry. I had very little money and no means of transportation so I spent a lot of time preparing for the Pathology test when we returned and bonding with Momma and Syl.

Pathology Exam

As promised, the first day back on Monday morning, we had the Pathology exam, consisting of having to view and report on microscopic Pathology slides, as well as a written exam.

I had prayed, prepared, and was pumped for the exam!

When the grades were posted on the Bulletin Board, which could be very demeaning for those whose scores were low or who failed, my score was 97!

One way to break a man's or woman's spirit is to have him or her fall from a perceived height of success to the lowest point of failure in one fell swoop. Dr. Horace Frazier, now deceased, burst my balloon the next day when in class he said because there had been too many good grades, he was throwing the test results out. This was great news to those who had not passed or had low scores.

This type of tyrannical teacher's response was an example of why there were many in our class who swore they would never give back to Meharry if and when they graduated. At that moment, I was tempted to feel that way...after all the preparation I had made during the Christmas Holidays to get ready for the test.

Thankfully, I got over that feeling, and I still try to pay my annual dues, and on many occasions, when we have the means, I do give more than my annual dues.

I would rather wear a robe of probity than a crown of niggardliness!

After the sophomore year, I was fortunate enough to get an Externship in Mound Bayou, Mississippi, at Taborian Hospital, described in more detail in the upcoming section on Mound Bayou.

The second part of my sophomore year after the devastating event of the Pathology exam scores being thrown out consisted of more direct contact with patients.

By the way, my final grade in Pathology was an "A".

The course Physical Diagnosis became the main event, as now we were taught how to take a good history and perform a good physical exam.

We had learned how to draw blood from each other, our buddy, and how to insert a nasogastric tube (NG) through the nose into the stomach, again on our buddy in our freshman year in Biochemistry.

I was smoking cigarettes at that time, about a pack a day, and trying to keep the NG tube in place for two hours was challenging. We collected the gastric aspirate (i.e., contents of the stomach, Chyme in medical terms) and then had to analyze the results, using the techniques we had learned in Biochemistry.

There was a very pretty cocoa-skinned female medical student in our class, whom I started calling Cholley. There were usually study Groups of three or four, teaming in some random manner, and we were in the same Group.

Cholley and I liked each other, but as I look back, we were concentrating on our studies and not so much on a social commitment. Several years later, after we had graduated, we met at a medical convention. She was married and an Anesthesiologist.

Easter Dinner

I do recall having met a very pretty young lady my freshman year, during the spring of 1960. She invited me to have Easter dinner with her family. I never offered any kind of emotional encouragement for long-term relations, I don't believe, to any of several women I would meet during my four years at Meharry, because I knew I wanted to concentrate on medicine.

The Easter meal was great, and afterward, I sincerely thanked the family for their hospitality and went to see the movie *The Ten Commandments* with Charleston Heston.

This was the first time I recall seeing a movie that had an intermission about halfway through, and this may have been the first such happening.

Years later, *Gone with the Wind* would be the next movie with an intermission.

I am sure I would see this movie at Easter time for the next twenty-plus years.

I remember walking to her home and to the movie, but I cannot remember ever seeing her again.

At the end of my sophomore year, several choice Externships were available. These were low-paying positions to work in a hospital assisting in any way the Physician decided. The positions were given at the whim of the staff and the senior residents.

There were lots of lonely days and nights during those four years. I often jogged during the day when the weather was not a deterrent, and only rarely can I remember playing tennis.

As it was, however, Ed Whitsey, now deceased, who was the number-one singles tennis player on our team at FAMU from 1949 to 1952, lived in Nashville, Tennessee. I had not seen Ed since he left FAMU in 1952. He had not been playing much tennis but was living at home with his mother. We did get to play on several occasions.

I wanted to become a Surgeon, and I made this known when we rotated through the Department of Surgery.

During my freshman year, I had thought about becoming a Psychiatrist, but after spending a day, 8:00 am to 5:00 pm locked in a psych ward, with staff and security, of course, I decided I really did not want to become a Psychiatrist. I knew I wanted to use my hands in medicine and recalled my last visit to Sacred Heart Catholic Church on NW Park Road in DC when I had prayed with my hands on the Crucifix at the front of the Church.

Mound Bayou, Mississippi

Again, The Lord made the decision, I believe, because I was the only student selected to go to Mound Bayou.[5] The town was originally started by Joseph E. Davis, brother of former Confederate President, Jefferson Davis. He intended to create a "model slave community" in 1887. According to two former slaves, Isaiah Montgomery and his cousin Benjamin Green were driving forces of establishing the town. It is said by Joseph Davis "a highly educated man, that slaves would work harder if educated." Isaiah Montgomery grew up on the Davis Hurricane Plantation at Davis Bend, twenty miles south of Vicksburg, and began his education at an early age, studying diligently, often in the extensive Davis family library.

An idea developed in his mind during this time to "want to develop a community unencumbered by racial handicaps imposed on us by the dying traditions of the past."

"In December 1887 Montgomery and Green bought 840 acres of land from the Louisianan-New Orleans & Texas Railroad for $7 an acre, the site of Mound Bayou." Only about seventy-five acres were immediately available for habitation. The rest of the land was covered by dense brush and trees and inhabited by bears, panthers, and snakes, and the danger of *swamp fever,* from which many died, was ever present.

During this time, there was no real understanding of what *swamp fever* was, its cause, or effective means of diagnosing or treating it. Today, we know that the term *swamp fever* refers to several diseases that may be caused by viruses or bacteria and are typically transmitted by mosquitoes— Malaria and West Nile virus being examples (*The Free Dictionary* by Farlex).

Montgomery and Green wanted Mound Bayou to be a sanctuary for Black families and Black culture for Blacks everywhere. Twelve Black former slave families were actively involved in the beginning, and by

---

[5] http://southernmemonesandupdtes.com/stories/first-all-black-town-inmississippi-found.

1907, a population of 4,000 people, 99.6 percent Black, occupied the town. There was a train depot, a Black post office, many churches, various industries, stores, a Negro newspaper, and eventually a hospital.

Cotton was the primary industry at the time, and many landowners in the area were former slaves. In the early 1900s, a fire destroyed much of the business district; however, the area again began to thrive in 1940. In 1942, members of the International Order of the Knights and Daughter of Tabor, with financial contribution from a White supporter, built the Taborian Hospital in Mound Bayou Mississippi. At the time, those interested paid $8.40 for adults and $1.20 for children, which entitled them to thirty-one days of hospitalization and a burial policy (*Mississippi Business Journal*, August 20, 2013).

I took the bus from Nashville to Mound Bayou, a distance of 313 miles. My living quarters were modest at best at the hospital, but that mattered little to me because I was about to start work as a "Doctor," in my mind. Since I was working primarily with the surgeons, and that was to be my chosen profession, my energies were directed to surgical procedures. One of my first assignments, as I recall, was to administer anesthesia to patients who were scheduled for operations and required" general Anesthesia". We had learned how to administer anesthesia by the "open drop" method in pharmacology. The word *anesthesia* was coined by Oliver Wendell Holder Sr. in 1846 from the Greek language (without sensation) referring to the inhibition of sensation (Wikipedia).

Crawford Long, a Physician and Pharmacist practicing in Jefferson, Georgia, administered diethyl ether to James Venable by inhalation to remove a tumor from his neck, and he is considered to be "The Father of modern anesthesia." I participated in numerous surgical procedures, including giving open-drop anesthesia to a number of patients.

I also witnessed my first Cesarean (C) section, the surgical procedure for delivering a baby.

Interestingly, all the women who delivered babies vaginally returned home within three or four hours. I had to write their discharge summaries, and I remember many saying they had to go back to the fields to *pick cotton*.

One of our Professors of Surgery at the time was Dr. Frank Perry (now deceased), and his brother, Father Harold Perry, was the first Colored Priest I had ever seen.

He also became the first Colored Bishop in the country. They were born in Lake Charles, Louisiana. The experience at Mound Bayou prepared me very well for my upcoming junior year at Meharry.

During this time, I was considering a residency in General Surgery or in Obstetrics and Gynecology (OB-GYN). My first rotation as a third-year student in September at Meharry was on OB-GYN.

Each student had to give a one-hour presentation to the class and faculty in the auditorium. The presentation would be a significant contribution to our grade.

Oral contraception was just coming to the forefront, so I decided that would be my presentation, "A Discussion of Oral Contraception." I had spent a considerable time preparing for my presentation, and I used the technique I had already learned in the army (i.e., using a lead pencil to draw my formula and key discussion parts on the blackboard). This was the same technique I discussed during my year in graduate school at Fisk in the Department of Chemistry. From my perspective, my presentation was spot-on, as I discussed the History, indications for use, and different brands and complications of oral contraceptives.

The Professor was not impressed, and my grade for the junior year was a D+.

Damn … another D+ and I did not know what I was not doing!

At the beginning of my junior year, I was still undecided between an OB-GYN or Surgery residency, despite the D+ in OB-GYN.

I had looked at various medical journals and noted that an Externship was available in the military in Takoma, Washington, during the summer. I had never been to that part of the country, and the pay looked good, so I applied and was accepted.

Externship

The Externship was provided through the US Army, and I reported as First Lieutenant Calhoun, in full military attire. My rotation was on OB-GYN.

During the Externship that summer, at Madigan General Hospital in Takoma, Washington, when I was not on duty, this was a very lonely experience. I was the only Negro male at the hospital. The other, my supervisor, was married and lived off base. When I sat at any table during breakfast, lunch, or dinner, I usually was not included in the conversations, though occasionally attempts would be made. I did not have the courage to start a conversation with any of the White Nurses away from the job area, and there were no Colored Nurses.

At the hospital, there were two cement tennis courts with a wall, and often, I would hit tennis balls against the wall as a means of exercise and enjoyment. On one occasion, I thought I recognized a White army Captain who had been the Coach of the tennis team when I practiced with the team in Fort Bliss, Texas, in 1954.

This was now the summer of 1962.

I recalled he had graduated from Purdue and was the Captain of the Purdue team. As he passed me hitting on the wall, he did not look over, and I did not call out to him …. who knows, was this was one of the effects of bigotry during this time or of my not being aggressive?

There was one occasion when I did meet another graduate from FAMU whose name I cannot recall. He was a Major, and one Saturday evening, we did drive into town in Takoma and slaked our thirst with a few beers, while recalling past incidents during our years at FAMU.

ATA Nationals

I finished the Externship around the end of July because I had entered the ATA Nationals and that would be the social highlight of the summer for me. I did not have a car, so I took a Greyhound bus to Xenia, Ohio, then to Central State College, where the tournament was held. This was the year I played doubles with Bobby Johnson, the son of "Whirlwind" Johnson, who was largely responsible for Arthur Ashe's tennis growth and development. Bobby and I had never played together, and as such, we did not have great teamwork. I believe we won a first-round match but lost in the next round.[6]

Years earlier, before medical school, I had met Dr. Johnson and asked him if I could train with his group. He told me I was too old. I was twenty one at the time and had been in the army, and he had only teenagers in his group.

When I returned to Nashville for our senior year, at some point, several of us rented a house a few blocks from campus. One of the guys was Bill Daniels. I am not sure who the other guys were.

The senior year was mainly rotating on the various medical floors and preparing for the final exams in Medicine, Surgery, OB-GYN, and Public Health. Everyone always passed the course in Public Health, we would find out, simply by attending the few lectures given by a Family Practice Physician from the local area. I don't remember his name. The course involved physical diagnosis, a major part of medicine we took the last semester of the junior year, so I was well prepared to examine patients.

Death at Graduation

Graduation Day was punctuated by a very sad experience. Word circulated around the campus that one of our classmates had been shot and killed by his wife that morning. Apparently, she had been supporting him financially during his training, but at graduation, he was planning to divorce her. None of the postmortem details were circulated.

On the positive side, Syl was able to attend graduation, having arrived the night before, and we drove back to Jacksonville after graduation.

Dr. Benjamin Mays, President of Morehouse College, gave the commencement address.

The last week before graduation, I had bought a white 1963 Chevy Impala from "Sarge," one of our classmates, who also was part owner of a car dealership. I had some money from the last of my GI Bill, and I would finish paying for the car during my Internship.

---

[6] Doug Smith, *Whirlwind: The Godfather of Black Tennis: The Life and Times of Robert Walter Johnson* (Blue Eagle Publishing, 2004).

Graduation was June 10, 1963, so I stayed in Jacksonville, relaxing with Syl and Momma until I left for Saint Louis, Missouri, for the Internship, reporting on July 1, 1963.

My brother Bill, had entered the Josephite Minor Seminary in New Burg, New York, as I noted earlier.

Sylvia (Syl)

As I said at the beginning, in the early years, my earliest memory of Syl, my biological mother, was her leaving to marry Walter Thompson, Bill's father, and my being pacified with a five-cent box of chocolate cookies.

I remember seeing Bill on his birthday, September 25, 1937, five years later, and being told he was my little brother.

As I grew older, I began to ask her questions about my birth.

She was not sure of her age and told me she was in the eighth grade at the time of my birth and had gone to "the fields to pick cotton" after school.

At the end of the day, she related, she returned home to find me "crying and lying in a pool of s..t with flies all around me." This is noted earlier.

She had no idea how long I had been like this she said. Tearfully, as she describes it, she washed me and the next day took what little money and clothes she had and we went to the Bus Station. She said she begged the bus driver to take what little money she had and take us to Jacksonville.

We were in Marianna, Florida, approximately 227 miles west of Jacksonville and the site of Blue Springs, one of the many Natural Springs in the state of Florida.

An unflattering fact about Marianna is that it was the site of "the White House Boys," a reform school where hundreds of boys, Black and White, were brutalized and many killed from the 1960s until the time it was closed on June 11, 2011.

When we arrived in Jacksonville, we went to Uncle Tom (Bud) and Luella Calhoun's house, as I have previously described.

Transportation and location of relatives during that time is a tall tale unto itself, the methodology of which I have little knowledge.

This is how I came to be named Tom Calhoun, as I described earlier.

Syl worked for most of her adult life, as I recall. She had her own café on several occasions along Ashley Street, which was the street where many Black owned business establishments flourished…note the three movie theaters, though they were not Black owned.

Bill tells me she was *an activist* before the term became popular. I recall she had a well-paying job at the Greyhound Bus Station in Jacksonville as the chief Cook. Apparently, business was good, and the White manager brought in a White lady and asked Syl to train her, presumably to replace her.

Syl said she quit that same day!

Syl was an attractive woman with long, silky black hair (see picture of her as an older woman). I only remember one other man in her life for a short period after her husband, Bill's father, died.

We heard that that he had been shot and killed some years earlier, but I do not have any of the surrounding circumstances.

The first time she met Shirley, Tom Junior, and Christine was when we took a trip to Jacksonville.

It would be several years later when she would meet Kathy and Maria, our other children.

Over the years, we communicated with letters and phone calls.

During the year before she died, we had been getting phone calls two and three times a week, and I began to think that all was not going well with Syl.

Although we never had seen a birth certificate for her, we, Bill and I, fixed her age in the mid-eighties.

One day we did get a phone call from a cousin in Jacksonville who told us Syl was in the Hospital. She indicated she would visit Syl several times a week, however, she had not done so recently. She related that she had gone to visit with her, but the door was locked, and upon looking in the window, she saw her lying on the floor. She always locked the doors and windows from the inside.

After police and fire broke into the house, she was taken to Brewster's Hospital, where Dr. Earl Cullins, one of the original Black Hawks, attended to her.

I called Earl, and he filled me in on her medical condition, and we were able to catch up on the years albeit, not under the best of circumstances.

When her condition stabilized and she was eating a regular diet, I brought her back to DC to our house at 4010 Argyle Terrace, NW.

With our four children still quite young and me now with a busy surgical practice, Shirley and I agreed that it would be best if we could find a nursing facility where she would receive the kind of twenty-four/seven care she needed.

Bill, who was now living in Columbia, Maryland, and I concurred, and he was able to find a facility in Ellicott, Maryland, about forty-five minutes from DC.

She seemed happy in that facility, and we visited her regularly.

I received an urgent call from the facility one evening and was told she was taken to the hospital because of severe "pain in the stomach." I contacted the emergency room at the Howard County General Hospital in Columbia, Maryland, the nearest hospital to the facility, and after identifying myself as her son and a General Surgeon, they explained that clinical findings and X-rays indicated she had a "perforated stomach ulcer."

This was pre-HIPAA (hhs.gov/hippa/for-professionals/privacy/index.html).

I told them to contact Dr. Jean Jacques, a General Surgeon whom I had helped train at Howard University and who was practicing at the facility.

Jean called me before surgery and again several hours later and told me she had a perforated gastric carcinoma (cancer), a not uncommon finding among elderly patients.

Some years earlier, she had told me, "If I get sick, I do not want all those tubes in my throat," which Bill and I interpreted to mean she was to have a *No Code* status if a health decision was needed. It was instituted.

On each occasion when I had visited her at the nursing facility, we always held hands and prayed a Rosary before I left, as we did each day after Surgery. (See "How to Pray the Rosary, 5 Million Rosaries"— Dynamic Catholic).

It was on the third postoperative day that we prayed the last Rosary. She seemed very much at peace when I left.

About forty-five minutes after I arrived home, I got the call from the hospital and was told "Your mother just died!"

What a blessing to have been allowed to pray a Rosary in those last moments!

CHAPTER 9
INTERNSHIP

In 1963, when we graduated from Meharry, or Howard University, there were only a few places in the country where we Colored graduates could go to receive a good postgraduate experience. Most of us did not want to stay another year at Meharry.

One of the choice places to go at that time was Homer G. Phillips Hospital in St. Louis, Missouri. There were two forms of Internships, one a straight Internship, the other a rotating Internship.

If an individual was pretty sure he or she wanted to become a particular type of specialist, Psychiatrist, for example, he or she would begin a straight internship for one year in the Department of Psychiatry and could feel pretty certain he or she would be selected as a first year resident in Psychiatry.

Although I did have some thoughts about becoming a Psychiatrist or an Obstetrics-Gynecology specialist, in the back of my mind, I wanted to become a Surgeon. A rotating internship was the preferred route for those interested in general surgery, and they did not have to compete with others for a position. There were four positions for a Surgery resident at Meharry and Howard, the only institutions, as previously mentioned, where a Black physician was more likely to be selected.

Homer G. Phillips, at that time, was considered *the flagship internship* for Negroes located in St. Louis, Missouri.

"The Hospital opened in1937 with 685 beds, six years after the assassination of Homer G. Phillips, a Saint Louis based African American Lawyer, who fought to gain a modern Hospital for the more than 70,000

African Americans in Saint Louis" (hgp). At that time, most (big) cities had a segregated system for health care, and as such, there was City Hospital 1 and City Hospital 2. Hospital 2, Homer Phillips, was located in the midst of the Negro community, whereas Hospital 1, which served Whites predominately, was in the most affluent section of the city.[7]

The St. Louis Cardinals with Hall of Fame players Stan "the Man" Musial, who was White, and later Bob Gibson, the famed Negro pitcher, as well as a professional basketball team were the main attractions in the city.

Curt Flood, another popular Negro player for the Saint Louis Cardinals, left the team and refused to play for a team to which he had been traded, rebuffing the *reserve clause* extant in baseball at the time. This clause essentially bound the player to the original team and ensured he had to go where he was traded.

The basketball team was one of the first to integrate and bring in a Black player, Cleo Hill, in 1961. He was much better than many of the White players; however, the unwritten rule was the Negro player could never outscore the White star, so often, he did not get very much playing time.

The primary reason Homer Phillips was thought of as a great place for an Internship was because of the variety of patients and illnesses. One rotated four months a year during the internship in the Department of Medicine, OB-GYN, and General Surgery. The Surgery rotation included Urology, Orthopedics/ Neurosurgery and Pathology. A fourth rotation included Psychiatry, in the Department of Medicine, and usually one took one's vacation, two weeks, during this rotation. A major part of the General Surgery rotation was for the intern to collect the X-rays of all the active Surgery patients, which was part of a discussion when the team, Intern, Residents, students, and faculty, made rounds and visited with each patient. Morning rounds usually started at 6:00 am with the sickest patients first and then those less so and those ready for discharge.

Depending on the number of patients on the surgical ward and the complexity of their problems, the senior residents would go to the Operating Room with the Attending Faculty Surgeon, leaving the junior Residents, Intern, and students to change dressings and write orders for

---

[7] hgp-http::/www.blackpast.org/?q=aah/homer-g-phillips-hospital-1937-1979.

the day, as well as make preparations for those being discharged with a discharge summary.

There were several highlights of my Internships worth noting.

Initially, when I arrived at Homer Phillips, I found out that there were only two of us, myself and another male from Howard. I remember speaking with the Hospital Director about hiring other Interns, and he said yes.

Bill Daniels (Dr. William Daniels, now deceased), who went to Howard undergrad and to Meharry, graduated with us. I was quite surprised when Bill said he was not going to do an Internship but was going back home to North Carolina. Bill, a very charismatic guy, had one of those *photographic minds,* and my roommate, Francis Baily Greene, now a Urologist practicing in Los Angeles and I would often allow him to come into our room from 2:00 to 4:00 am to read our notes.

There was no requirement to attend classes starting the junior year, but one had to pass the exams. Most of the class, some seventy-plus students, six of whom were female, knew Bill Daniels and each other very well. In fact, the class was for the most part very supportive of each other. Although internships began on July 1, usually things did not settle down until July 5, after the July 4 holiday. Even today, most teaching medical facilities make additional arrangements to cover the last week in June and the first week in July during this week of change. At any rate, I called Bill at his home in North Carolina and told him the hospital would hire him as an Intern, and he did come.

Later, Bill went into the US Army, completed a residency in psychiatry, and had a very successful practice in Montgomery County, Maryland. He died of a heart attack in the 1980s.

A big event Bill and I debated was attending the March to DC for the Martin Luther King Jr. speech in DC in August of 1963. We talked about it a few days before the event, but since we had just started our Internships a few weeks earlier, we decided that we would not attend.

I wish now we had gone!

The next big event occurred on November 22, 1963, about 1:30 p.m. eastern standard time.

I had been on duty for the past twenty-four hours and grabbed a couple of sandwiches, some fruit, and a soda from the dining room and returned to my room in the Intern Quarters.

I turned on my twenty-one-inch black-and-white television, and within minutes, I was seeing and hearing the news that President Kennedy had just been shot and was in critical condition!

I am sure I began praying for his speedy recovery. At that time, there was no news of the severity of the condition.

Later in the day, he was pronounced dead at Parkland Hospital in Dallas, Texas, on November 23, 1963.

This was an event that shook the conscience of the country and perhaps beyond.

Years later, the primary surgeon who attended President Kennedy when he was brought to Parkland Hospital visited us at the Department of Surgery at Howard University and related his experiences associated with that fated occasion.

Another scary experience was an encounter with a patient in the throes of alcohol withdrawal. Aluminum poles were at the bedsides for hanging fluids that were administered intravenously. On one occasion, I was changing his fluids, and he suddenly grabbed the pole and came charging at me. I ran, and immediately orderlies on the ward stopped him and he was carefully sedated.

The Hoodlum Priest

Velma was a very attractive middle-aged female Secretary who worked in the Office of Administration at Homer Phillips Hospital. Whenever one passed the office, she was readily noticed.

Word was she was a *special friend* of the Chief of Surgery, Dr. A. S., now deceased,... translation, "Do not hit on her"!

As I had done throughout my adult life, after I moved to a new area, one of the first things I did was find the location for the nearest Catholic church.

Saint Francis Xavier was about a ten-minute drive from the hospital, and the Pastor was a Jesuit Priest, Father Charles Dismas.

I had heard about Father Dismas and the Dismas House from the movie *The Hoodlum Priest*, which was released in March 1961. Prior to attending Mass at St. Xavier, I visited Dismas House and introduced myself to the Priests. Funds to build Dismas House were raised in part because of a special musical appearance put on by Frank Sinatra and the Rat Pack with Sammie Davis Jr. and Dean Martin.

I attended Mass every Sunday at St. Xavier and would often speak with some of the Priests after Mass.

Lent is considered the holiest part of the year for Catholics and includes Holy Thursday, Good Friday and Holy Saturday, on which there are no Masses, and Easter Sunday. On Monday, Tuesday and Wednesday I went to 6:30 am Mass. On each of those days after Mass, only a few were in attendance, I had short conversations with the Priests so I was well known by them.

There were evening services on Holy Thursday and Good Friday, but no services or Vigil Mass on Saturday at that time.

As I noted earlier, I was well aware that Velma (I cannot recall her last name) was a *special friend* of Dr. A. S., and as such, I had never had a conversation with her, other than a polite, cordial greeting.

Sometime in the spring of 1964, Velma called me!

Whoa! I was blown away … with no idea where this came from or where it was going! It was known that she was not married and that Dr. A. S. was. She essentially asked me for a date, which I immediately agreed to. No way was I not going to! I asked her what brought this on, and she said she had been driving behind me one evening, and I ignored her. Truth be told, I had *not* seen her, but she decided to follow up on the event. We agreed on dinner at a nice restaurant, not too upscale, as my salary as an intern was 90 dollars a month, a place she selected, as Saint Louis was her hometown. She suggested we have Caesar's salads. It was the first time I had eaten one, and I love them to this day. We also had Prime Rib, which at that time was within the range of my paycheck! (See footnote for the origins of the Caesar's salad!)[8]

We dated several times before the end of the Internship on June 30, the last time on a Friday evening.

---

[8] From Wikipedia, Caesar Cardini, an Italian immigrant restaurant owner on July 4, 1925, in Tijuana, Mexico, introduced the Caesar's salad.

Ray Charles had a big hit song at that time, "What'd I say," and one of the verses was "see the girl with the red dress on"!

Velma was fair-skinned with reddish-brown hair and hazel eyes and was very well built. She wore a red dress that evening, and the word *stunning* seems almost blasphemous in describing how she looked!

We went to a frequently visited honkytonk club in East Saint Louis, Illinois, just across the state line, early to get a table. The term honkytonk now describes a club where country music is played. Not so in 1964! Then it was where rhythm and blues was played. We had dinner consisting of fried chicken, collard greens, black-eyed peas, corn bread, and sweet potato pie and danced the night away. I am sure we had drinks. Scotch and soda was a favorite, although I drank my Scotch with milk.

We left the club sober around midnight, and I drove Velma home. While parked outside her house, I was opening the car door on the passenger side for her to exit when a car came speeding up beside us, and Dr. A. S. got out, screaming some obscenities, and threw a punch at me but missed! I had the sense after it was over that he intended to miss. Then he left, speeding away in his car. Both Velma and I were quite shaken up emotionally, but no physical harm had been done, and I escorted her to her door.

Driving back to the Hospital to my room, I made the decision that I would not pursue the issue, rather, if you would, again, to wear a crown of probity rather than a robe of parsimony or niggardliness!

I was very disappointed by Dr. A. S.'s actions because I had had a lot of respect for him. I recall on morning rounds one day with him, he said to me, "Calhoun, a Surgeon must be a supreme egotist"! I did not fully agree with him, reflecting on my Catholic upbringing and the Church's teaching that one must always keep pride in check.

Years later, that phrase came to mind as I wrote in "The Surgeon's Prayer" (see herewith), "To be able to lay on our fellowman the cold blade of the steel scalpel or the heat of the cautery, without fear or intimidation, and remove diseased flesh, created by you, does not come from man, but surely the promptings of the Holy Spirit."

Another phrase I also remember was often spoken by LaSalle D. Leffall Jr., MD, deceased, the former Chair of the Department of Surgery,

Howard University, Washington DC (see *No Boundaries: A Cancer Surgeon's Odyssey*, Howard University Press, 2005): "equanimity under duress."

This phrase has served me well as a surgeon and also as a man. In other words, whatever the occasion, don't lose your cool! This is really a concise description of the *Rubaiyat of Omar Khayyam*, which I noted during the discussion of my freshman year.

With about two weeks left before the end of the Internship, I did not want to do anything that might jeopardize my completing it, so I said nothing about the event, nor did Velma and I date again before I left.

The following week, there was a rumor that I would not be given my certificate for completion of the Internship because I had been seen having *illicit sexual relationships with boys*!

Whoa … Where did this come from?

Someone wanted to spread calumny about me, describing me as *a profligate*, teeming with *opprobrium*!

I am sure I prayed about it, and then I called St. Xavier and spoke with one of the Priests with whom I was familiar. I related the accusation to him…it was completely untrue of course…and he told me not to worry, he would take care of it.

Dismas House did have a working relationship with a well-known group of Attorneys in the area.

Sugar in the Gas Tank

I was off duty the Saturday before the Internship ended and had decided to go to Forest Park and play tennis on one of the many red-clay courts. I did not have anyone to play with but felt pretty sure I would find an opponent, which I did. I had stopped at a Gulf Oil Gas Station before arriving at the park to have my oil checked and get a full tank of gas.

The gas attendant said, "Hey, did you know your gas tank has sugar in it?"

Was this a macabre or heinous act or a combination of both?

Sugar does not dissolve in gas as it does in water but may crystallize in the tank, and depending upon the amount, it could potentially ruin an engine.

I left the car and was able to find someone to play tennis with, and when I returned several hours later, the fuel line had been drained and the tank filled.[9]

Certificates were scheduled to be given out on Tuesday morning June 30, starting at 9:00 am. I went to pick up my certificate at 9:00 a.m. and was told it was not ready but to come back at 9:30. I did and picked up my certificate.

I suspect a call had come from the Priest with whom I had spoken or the Law firm associated with the Dismas House.

I left immediately for Washington DC to begin a residency in General Surgery.

CHAPTER 10
THE RESIDENCY

Following a rotating internship at the now closed Homer G. Phillips Hospital in St. Louis, Missouri, I began a four-year surgical residency at Freedmen's Hospital, Howard University, in Washington DC on July 1, 1964.

My first rotation was in the Department of Pathology. The day ended at 5:00 pm, and I was "on call" for any patients who presented to the emergency room with a surgical problem and patients admitted by the surgical attending physician, or any Surgery Consultations required that night.

First Operation at Howard

One such patient even today, fifty years later, remains vivid in my mind. A young female, six months pregnant, was admitted by Dr. Leffall, who was an Attending Surgeon in the Department at that time. Her diagnosis was Acute Appendicitis, and she was prepared for surgery that evening.

Dr. Lasalle D. Leffall Jr. was an alumnus of my alma mater FAMU and also a fraternity brother, an Alpha. This was my first time in the OR with any of the Attending Surgeons, so I wanted "to shine," as it were.

After the patient was asleep, under general anesthesia, and prepped, I became somewhat unnerved when Dr. Leffall gave me the scalpel and told me to make the incision. I knew my anatomy, and after a few deep breaths, I proceeded to start to make an incision in the right lower quadrant of the abdomen, where 99 percent of appendices are located normally.

In one percent or less of humans, the Appendix may be located in another position, the left lower quadrant, or when the patient has *situs inversus*, organs are reversed or transposed left to right.

Before I made the incision, Dr. Leffall said, "Remember, she is six months pregnant!"

So much for shining! Dr. Leffall took the scalpel and made the incision in the right upper abdomen, where the acutely inflamed appendix was located and swiftly and deftly removed it.

The patient did well and was discharged several days later.

During this time, patients were kept in the hospital often five to seven days before discharge, and hospitals were paid for those days.

I had forgotten that during pregnancy, the internal organs are displaced by the enlarged pregnant Uterus.

The first three months, July, August, and September, were rotations through the Departments of Pathology, Orthopedics/Neurosurgery and Urology, assisting in a number of operations in the latter two departments. Orthopedics and Neurosurgery were covered by the same General Surgery Resident; however, Orthopedics also had its own Residents.

District of Columbia (DC) General Hospital

In January 1965, I began a six-month rotation at the District of Columbia (DC) General Hospital, located in Southeast DC. DC General was established as the Washington Infirmary in 1806 and having gone through several name iterations over the ensuing years, officially closed as the only Public Hospital in the District of Columbia on October 30, 2018. It provided services primarily for the African American residents in the District who were uninsured. Later, after review of hospital records, it was found that "60 percent of admissions were self-insured"; however, these funds were never collected.

DC General received most of the gunshot injuries and other trauma victims in the Metropolitan area, and as such, the word was for any trauma victim, take them to DC General where a high level of expertise had been attained.

Current trauma centers, such as the Washington Hospital Center, had not been established. There were three Surgery programs at DC General at this time of overt segregation in the country; Georgetown and George Washington Universities and Howard.

To try to recount some of the injustices and inequalities of the health care provided at that time at DC General Hospital would require volumes unto themselves.

Shirley Jones and I had been corresponding with letters since the summer of 1965. She visited with me and stayed at one of the guest rooms at DC General, at no charge because I was training there. After several days of meeting with some of my friends, playing tennis, and seeing some of the sights, I flew back to California with her and met her parents.

DC General, as a Hospital, closed in 2018, as previously noted, and became a homeless shelter for 270 families.

The summer of 1965 was memorable in another very significant event.

The National Public Parks Clay Tennis Championships were held here in DC at the Sixteenth and Kennedy Fitzgerald Tennis Facility in the summer of 1965. One of the entrants was Shirley Jones with whom I had corresponded over the past year as I noted. She lost her singles match in the semifinals to the eventual winner and was a doubles finalist. We were able to have several dinner dates during the week she was here.

She was teaching high school in Long Beach, California, and I invited her to come to DC for a few days in the summer of 1966, as I note above.

We would marry, as noted later in the book.

The remainder of my first and second years of the residency was filled with numerous medical experiences, affording me continuing growth and development. The third year of the residency came with more managerial responsibility, primarily as regarded the Interns and Medical Students who rotated with us, as well as the first- and second-year Residents.

In 1968, two ex-military Black males approached the Howard University Surgery Department here at DC General with the request to venture in to a new medical concept, that of Physician's Assistants.

By our assessment these were sincere, motivated young men, and the Chairman decided to take part in their request.

They had been denied their request by several other medical facilities in DC.

There was no official description for a Physician Assistant in the country at that time and no Official License for this discipline was available.

They had extensive medical training in the Military, along with Military Physicians and Nurses, so we decided to allow them to work alongside our Surgical Residents, without any payment, for three months.

They were allowed to do minor suturing of wounds, changes surgical dressings, draw blood, start intravenous lines, all with supervision, and they attended formal lectures and conferences that were provided.

Their performance as outstanding!

In 1969, they began work in the Emergency Department at George Washington (GW)Hospital here in DC, and in 1970, a formal program for Physician Assistants was established at GW.

Some years later, one of the young men became Chairman of the Program, which is now one of the outstanding Programs in the country.

Myriad Operations

With the number of operations` I performed at DC General Hospital, one especially comes to mind. One had to verify having performed at last fifty major operations by completion of Residency. At this point, I had well over 150.

A mother presented her five- or six-year-old (not sure of the age) child to us at the Surgery Clinic with the tip of his second finger, right hand, which had accidentally been severed shortly before they arrived. The finger-tip and the finger, were wrapped in cloth.

After evaluation and discussion with the Chief of Surgery, we made the decision to reattach the fingertip. We told the mother we did not know if it would be successful. After considering the circumstances…a recent event, less than an hour, a growing child…and the team following the necessary sterile procedures and with appropriate anesthesia, we completed the reattachment, with a small splint to prevent bending of the finger during healing.

The child was seen at one, two, and three weeks after the procedure with no complications and healing going well, and sutures were removed. He was discharged and Mom told to follow up if problems occurred.

About a year later, I was at Freedmen's Hospital and I felt a tug on my long, white lab coat, and looking down, I saw a smiling youngster with a finger, bending and pointing up at me. It was the youngster and his Mom, both smiling and asking if I remembered him, which I did.

The reimplantation was successful!

The year was 1967, and how often thereafter I wished I could have been prescient enough to see the future of organ transplantation!

Norfolk Community Hospital

WEDDING

I spent the first six months on a rotation at Norfolk Community Hospital in Norfolk, Virginia. A third-year resident in OB-GYN, Donald S. (now deceased), was also rotating, and the two of us were responsible for all the surgery performed at the hospital for this period, of course with Attending Physicians' supervision.

I did play tennis on occasions during this time and experienced a not uncommon event of "Jim Crowism" for us Negroes. I entered a men's tennis tournament at the local Country Club. I sent the appropriate entry blank, entry fee, and proof of my being a member of the US Lawn Tennis Association as required. Several days later, I received my scheduled playing time in the mail, and I arrived at the Club for my first match.

To my dismay, somewhat, when I parked and began walking toward the Club with my tennis gear, a young White male came rushing out to meet me and tell me they had not received my entry. I told them I had received my time to report, but he said there was some mistake—in other words, Negroes could not play! I was not prepared to contest the decision at the time and left. I asked for my entry fee of twenty-five dollars to be returned. I cannot recall if it ever was.

I returned to DC with my last six months at DC General Hospital.

During this time, my relationship with Shirley had become one of deep and profound love, and we exchanged many letters.

I had asked her to marry me the previous summer at the ATA National Tennis Tournament at Central State. She said yes, and on Saturday,

December 2, 1967, we were wed at St. Anthony's Catholic Church in Long Beach, California.

I was Chief Resident and had received the best wishes and congratulations of many of the members of the Surgery Department.

We left sunny California's eighty-degree temperatures and returned to DC to snow and temperatures in the low thirty degrees, but alas, we were in love!

As of this writing, come December 2, 2021, God willing, we will have been married for fifty-four years.

Completion of Residency

In September of 1968, I began a Fellowship in Thoracic and Cardiovascular surgery at Freedmen's Hospital.

Having completed my residency in June, I was without any incoming funds for July and August.

I borrowed $600 from Dr. Erwin Edgecombe, deceased. I had met him years earlier at the junior tennis tournament I played in West Palm Beach, Florida, in 1948. Dr. Edgecombe was one of the Attending Surgeons at Howard who helped train me.

He told me I did not have to repay him.

Also, I *moonlighted, outside work while still in training,* in the office with Dr. Andrew B. (now deceased) and could treat patients whom I saw during that time and bill for any procedures, a practice at this time, if surgery was required. When we left California after the wedding, we lived on Mount Pleasant Street in Northwest DC, near Sacred Heart Catholic Church on Sixteenth and Park Road Northwest, where I regularly attended Mass when I was in DC.

It became our Parish Church.

Martin Luther King Jr. Assassination

One of the most dramatic events of the time was the assassination of Dr. Martin Luther King Jr. on April 4, 1968. I recall Shirley and a friend, Doris, driving in the Mount Pleasant area during the time US Army tanks were patrolling the area. I had to walk from Freedmen's Hospital to our Apartment, about two miles away.

Shirley was pregnant with our first child at the time, and during this time, we had our first argument.

How could she be out driving at a time like that while pregnant?

She had met a friend Doris, who was married but with no children, and they were "sight seeing".

I should have remembered that Shirley was twenty-four years old and had been single and accustomed to doing what she wanted to do. She was used to driving to many places throughout the country to various tennis tournaments.

The argument was soon resolved and she agreed it was unwise to continue, so she stopped. We moved to a town house at 54 G Street Southwest, where Thomas Calhoun Jr. was born. Two years later, Christine René was born, and later, another daughter, Kathyrne (Kathy) Yvonne was born. With the birth of Kathy, we moved to 4010 Argyle Terrace Northwest (NW).

CHAPTER 11
4010 ARGYLE TERRACE

SHIRLEY

Shirley was born in Charlestown, West Virginia, on June 21, 1943, the oldest girl in a family of eight, four boys and four girls. By her account, she was tomboyish until age twelve. Her father worked in the US Post Office in Charlestown, West Virginia, and coached on the side. She says she had to train with the boys, playing basketball and shortstop in soft ball, and climbed trees with the boys.

She was the playground paddle tennis champ and developed an interest in tennis at the urging of the White playground director, Hugh Thompson Jr.

Her tennis improved, and later, she won the West Virginia Junior Girl's Championship and the Womens Singles Championship.

She was the first and, to date, the only African American to win the West Virginia State Tennis Championship.

After high school, she was awarded a tennis scholarship to Central State College, from which she graduated with a Bachelor of Science degree in Education on June 7, 1964.

Prior to attending Central State College, she played one year on the men's tennis team at West Virginia State. (See pictures).

She joined the Delta Sigma Theta sorority and was named an All American in Volleyball, Basketball, and Tennis at Central State College.

It was in high school that she met Althea Gibson and Pancho Gonzales, well-known tennis Champions in their own right, and both are mentioned in other parts of the book.

She received a Master of Science degree in Physical Education from the University of California at Los Angeles (UCLA) in 1966.

We postponed a honeymoon until I completed my residency and celebrated it a few years later with a trip to the Greenbrier Country Club in West Virginia. Our firstborn was Thomas Calhoun Jr., born October 2, 1968, weighing eight and a half pounds.

He would be left-handed—an asset in sports, some think.

Next, as mentioned, was Christine, who developed an interest in music early. She was born January 29, 1970. Then came Kathryne (Kathy), the academic one, named after Shirley's mother. She was born on my birthday, October 6, but in 1971. My year of birth is 1932.

Kathy had blue-green eyes at birth, but over time, they became a light green. She enjoyed reading and was an English major in College. We discussed studying Law as a career, but she said no. Instead, she has a Master's degree in Human Resources from the University of Maryland. Later, she became a Certified Pharmacy Technician.

Christine, who also has a Master's degree in Applied Management from the University of Maryland, works as a procurement analyst in the Copyright Division of the Federal Government in Washington DC.

Tom Junior, after a year in the University of Maryland school system, pursued a semiprofessional career in tennis and then married and now has four children.

Tom became ill with bipolar disorder in 2005 and is still struggling with the condition.

Maria was born on June 10, 1975. She was the charismatic one who liked to give big hugs.

All of the children went to Catholic Schools from first through eighth grade.

Tom Junior graduated from the Catholic St. John's College High and Kathy from the Georgetown Visitation, the all-girls Catholic school. Christine and Marie graduated from public schools, all here in DC.

Shirley, taught at the elementary levels in DC.

On Monday afternoon, August 18, 2003, Maria gave me a big hug, and that was the last time I saw her alive.

Maria was killed in a hit-and-run accident on August 19, 2003, in route to Barry College in Miami, Florida. She was twenty-eight (see picture).

After Thomas and Christine were born, we knew we had to move to a larger place.

As it happened, we were working with a Realtor from Shannon's and Luck's, a popular Real Estate Agency at the time, who contacted us after we had been playing tennis one Sunday afternoon to show us a house.

We were shown 4010 Argyle Terrace NW in DC. We met the owner, a retired White Navy Admiral, and his wife. He told me he had cancer after I told him I was a Surgeon.

We noted a tennis racquet on his wall and told him we had just finished playing tennis, and after a several minutes of conversation, he said, "The house is yours"!

Before we moved to 4010, Dr. Charles Clark, now deceased, who was also a General Surgeon and Attending Surgeon at Howard, who lived near the house, called me one day and told me the house had been struck by lightning!

I drove by and noted that the east side of the third floor was open to the elements because of the lightning strike. Fortunately, the previous owners' home insurance paid for all the repairs. Before we moved in, I asked an Architect friend of mine to inspect the house for us, which he did, free of charge, and indicated there were no structural damages caused by the lightning.

We bought the house for $55,000 then in1972, and when we sold it in 2015, the price was over $950.00.

Free of Charge

The lightning strike on the house was not the only concern we had when we were moving to 4010. After the birth of Christine and Kathy, each had yellowing of their eyes (yellow jaundice), and at the time, there was the concern that they may have a condition called Kernicterus.

Kernicterus is a condition in some young infants with yellowing of the eyes and skin and may lead to brain damage. In most cases, the jaundice disappears in a few days as the infant's Liver develops and is able to remove the Bilirubin (BR) formed during the normal breakdown of Red Blood Cells and excreted in the urine responsible for the yellowish color.[10]

In our case, this and other events resulted in Shirley developing a severe case of postpartum depression for which she had to be hospitalized for several weeks at a local hospital here in DC.

This was at the same time I was scheduled to take the second part of my surgery boards, the oral part, for fellowship into the American College of Surgery. On the day I was to leave for New York City, where the exam was to be given, Shirley thought I was leaving her. I tried to reassure her that I was just going for the day to take the exam and would return the same afternoon. She was unable to understand and developed *vocal paralysis* so she was unable to talk. I discussed this with the Nurses and Doctors, all of whom agreed this was likely temporary, but when I left, I had the thought that perhaps I should postpone the exam.

I took the train to New York along with Dr. Horace Lassiter, a Surgery Resident whom we had trained at Howard (now deceased) and who was also taking the exam.

I received the letter two weeks later that I did not pass. Horace and I both failed the exam, and I wondered if I had made a mistake in going because on the train returning to DC, while recalling the questions asked, I knew all of the answers!

I did take the exam the following year, the earliest time a repeat exam could be taken, and passed quite easily.

Some years later, oral exams were discontinued as a part of the Surgery Boards, having been deemed too subjective with the penalty of having to wait an entire year before a repeat exam could be taken.

Shirley did fully recover, and we had couples therapy for six months. We have now been married for fifty-three years, our anniversary being on December 2, 2020.

Our therapist, a Catholic Priest who was also a Psychiatrist (now deceased), often had dinner at our home afterward.

---

[10] en.wikipedia.org/wiki/Bilirubin.

Instructor, Department of Surgery

I began work as an Instructor in the Division of Cardiothoracic Surgery at Freedmen's Hospital, Howard University, and would advance to the position of Assistant Chief of Surgery at DC General Hospital in 19742 and Associate Professor of Surgery, Department of Surgery, at Howard University in 1974.

In the early 1980s, in the medical community, there was a movement away from training programs in non-university-affiliated hospitals. In order for the program to be approved by the medical governing bodies, all training programs in Medicine and Surgery had to be *integrated* with a teaching university.

One such program was present at Providence Hospital, a Catholic Hospital in northeast Washington DC, which had received its initial charter from President Abraham Lincoln.

It had been my plan and hope that after I completed my training, I would work in a Catholic Hospital. By doing so, I reckoned, I could go to daily Mass and more actively practice my Catholic faith.

The major obstacle to that plan at the time was segregation. Although Cardinal Patrick O'Boyle had desegregated Catholic schools and churches in DC in 1951, three years before the Supreme Court decision of 1954, the spirit of segregation remained.

I was the third Black surgeon given admitting and surgical privileges at Providence.

Admitting Privileges, Providence Hospital

Although I was fully board certified by the American Board of Surgery, it would take me a year to get privileges. One of the requirements was to meet with the Chairman of the Department, and his secretary never would or could fit me into his schedule.

It happened that one afternoon, I was raking leaves in our backyard at 4010 and looking over the fence, and whom do I see? None other than Dr. Louis Goffredi (now deceased), the Chairman of the Department of

Surgery at Providence. Our backyards abutted each other. We had lived in such close proximity for over a year, both unaware, I assumed.

His words were when he saw me were, "Oh hi, do you live here"?

I said yes, and some neighborly conversation followed.

The next day, I was given privileges at Providence. It was September 1970.

Although I was able to admit patients and operate at Providence, many instances of racism were still rampant, such as often being ignored or shut out of conversations in the Doctors' lounge.

President, Medical and Dental Staff

There were some positive changes, however, such as my being elected as President of the Medical and Dental staff in 1997, some twenty-five years after I was granted admitting privileges.

Another pleasant event included being invited to the farm in nearby Maryland by of one of the urgeons, Dr. Al Sarachi (deceased), for his annual outing. The picture of our youngest daughter, Maria, and me at the farm brings back fond memories (ss image).

Another big thrill for Shirley and me was a visit to the Greenbrier in West Virginia as I was President of the Medical and Dental staff, and the Executive Committee from Providence traveled there for a retreat. Shirley was born in Charleston, West Virginia, and indicated she had never thought she would get to visit the Greenbrier!

The social highlight of the retreat was the twelve-course dinner… absolutely *obsequious*!

Chief of Clinical Surgery

In 1981, I proposed that Providence get an affiliation with Howard University, and when both Hospitals agreed, I became the Chief of Clinical Surgical Services and the Integrated Surgical Residency Program between Providence and Howard. Initially, there was still nonacceptance of the Residents from Howard and me by the Surgery Staff; soon, however, there was general acceptance.

ATA Nationals in Jackson, Mississippi

Over the years, after I became a General Surgeon, Harold Freeman and I met at various surgical meetings, and on one occasion, we played tennis. The last time was in August 1990 in Atlanta, Georgia, during the American College of Surgery's Annual Meeting.

That year was memorable for me in another way. After the meeting in Atlanta, Shirley and I flew to Jackson, Mississippi, where I had entered the ATA National Tournament in the men's 70 singles and with Jim Ridgley (now deceased) in the doubles.

In the semifinals against Marcel Freeman (now deceased), the score was 1-2, 15-30 on my serve in the first set. Just after my first serve, I heard a popping sound, which distracted me. I looked around to see what had happened, and after a few steps, I noticed my right foot was not moving properly. As I took a few more steps, it became clear: I had popped my right Achilles Tendon. The popping sound was classic, just as it is described in Surgery textbooks, but I did not experience any pain.

The Tendon is named after the mythical Greek warrior Achilles, whose tendon was allegedly struck by an arrow.

The popping meant the Achilles tendon came off the bony or calcaneal attachment to the heel. The tendon is the largest tendon in the body but has a poor blood supply. It's the most common one to rupture. As one ages, the tendon thickens. If that rupture had involved the muscular attachment, a few centimeters higher on the calf, the pain would have been quite severe.

Looking back now on the event, as I have done on many occasions, I remember I had deliberately made an incorrect call on a ball my opponent had hit. He had lobbed the ball over my head, which I called out, but which I could see, was in. Even on looking closer at the spot, which is always left playing on clay, or Har-Tru, the surface we were playing on, I clearly saw the spot I had called the out...in other words, I cheated!

This was out of character as I noted during the earlier years, referring to tennis decorum, which Chip Reed had taught me as a teenager, was to always give the opponent the point if we were not sure.

Moreover, in this case, I was winning the match rather easily!

I think the Lord allowed my injury as punishment for my cheating. That was on a Wednesday morning.

That afternoon, I was able to get to Jackson Memorial Hospital, where the Chief of Surgery was a former Surgery Resident I had helped train at Howard, and the first African American Chief of Surgery at Jackson Memorial, in Mississippi of all places!

At the time, he could not see me personally, but he sent the Chief Resident to see me.

He did see me later that evening and told me that the Hospital was being reviewed by the Joint Commission for Accreditation of Hospitals (JCAH), and he was involved.

We agreed that Surgery would be necessary to reattach the tendon.

I was not going to have the operation away from home, an elective, non-emergent procedure, so the Chief Resident applied a soft plaster cast.

Shirley and I were able to get a flight out of Jackson the next day, Thursday afternoon.

When we arrived back in DC, I was able to contact Dr. Major Gladden Jr. (now deceased), at his home, and that Friday morning, he reattached the tendon. I never had any significant pain, taking only a couple of Tylenol with codeine as needed.

I had scheduled two operations the following Monday morning, which I could not afford to cancel. After surgery, Major applied a fiberglass walking boot, and I was able to drive with no problems. For my operations, after I had scrubbed and gowned, the Operating Room Nurse had a rolling chair, which I used, and the cases went well, both laparoscopic cholecystectomies (i.e., removal of diseased Gall Bladders by the minimally invasive technique).

After three months, I was healed and playing tennis again.

I saw Dr. Harold Freeman again several years later in Nashville, Tennessee, in August when the National Medical Association (NMA) held its annual meeting. The NMA is the predominately African American Association formed some one hundred years ago, because the Colored Doctors were not accepted by the White medical societies.

Ironically, this would be the last time I saw Dr. Earl Thomas Cullins. Looking at him, I knew he was very ill, and as it turned out, he did expire the following year from complications of Parkinson's disease. Harold and I met again here in DC some years later for the funeral services of his niece

Vicky, who had died in her early fifties and later in 2019, for the funeral of Ben Metz, who had expired because of Prostate Cancer.

I am writing another Book entitled, "43, A SURGEON'S WAKE UP CALL", about my Prostate Cancer, which I hope to publish soon.

Pilgrimage to Medjugorje (Between the Hills)

It was late Friday afternoon when I finished the operation at Capitol Hill Hospital in northeast DC, a partial resection of the stomach for a chronically obstructed ulcer. After writing the appropriate postoperative orders and speaking with the relatives of the patient, I left for home. The next morning, Saturday, I visited the patient at Capitol Hill Hospital, now long since closed, and the other two patients I had there, and all were doing well. Again, I wrote the appropriate orders and progress notes.

I had been having some trouble with my back, so I went straight home to relax.

I was awakened Sunday morning with the urge to urinate, and to my astonishment, I had to crawl to the bathroom because of severe back pain.

I woke Shirley and told her I needed to get to the Emergency Room. We went to Providence Hospital, where my office was located.

I contacted Dr. Edward "Tony" Rankin, Chief of Orthopedic Surgery, and was admitted to the hospital with a diagnosis of *severe back pain*. After three days of heat, ultrasound, muscle relaxants, bed rest and pain meds, I was discharged, improved, to continue with heat, the same medications, a stool softener, and rest at home.

Earlier in the week, I had picked up a book by Wayne Weible titled *Medjugorje: The Message* (1989).

Reader's Digest, a popular magazine, had reported some time earlier of six young children in Medjugorje, Bosnia-Herzegovina, Yugoslavia, who allegedly had been seeing and talking with the Virgin Mary, whom we Catholics, and others, believe was the Mother of Jesus Christ.

One afternoon, while I was recovering at home, lying in bed and reading the book, my brother, Bill, called from New York and told me that he and Mary, his wife, were at JFK Airport in route to Medjugorje. I could not believe the coincidence.

Years earlier, Bill had been in the Josephite Seminary preparing to become a Catholic Priest, and Mary had been in a Convent preparing to become a Catholic Nun, as I noted previously.

This was the day Nelson Mandela was freed from 27 years in prison, February 11, 1990.

I improved and resumed work, but I decided then and there, that one day I would go to Medjugorje

On June 20, 1996, I arrived at Dulles International Airport (IAD) in Chantilly, Virginia, at 3:30 p.m. and reported to the Lufthansa check-in area.

I had booked my flight, nonstop, to Split Croatia, an independent country, which had seceded from Yugoslavia in 1991. It is located on the eastern shore of the Adriatic Sea, linked to the Adriatic Islands and Apennine Peninsula (Wikipedia).

I was part of a group of pilgrims going to Medjugorje. We had met at St. Thomas Aquinas Catholic Church in Baltimore, Maryland, two weeks earlier and were given an overview of the trip and expectations by Father George Restrepo, a Catholic Jesuit Priest. He had been to Medjugorje seven times and told us, among many other firsthand facts, and that we should be prepared to experience a wide range of feelings and emotions.

Although I had promised myself that I would not expect to witness any miracles, I did want to be open to whatever experiences occurred. One of the first such experiences happened on the bus ride from the Airport to Martin's House in Medjugorje, where we would be staying.

I heard a shriek from the rear of the bus and one of the ladies saying, "Look! My rosary has turned to gold!" She passed the rosary forward for each of us to see. Perhaps in keeping with my name, Thomas (Doubting), since I had not seen the original rosary, my reaction was sort of so-so.

The next day, we visited Apparition Hill, where the Blessed Mother first appeared to the young children on June 24, 1981.

Apparition Hill, Podbrdo in Croatia, is about 640 feet above sea level. For a relatively healthy individual, it takes about twenty minutes to walk to the top of the hill, and on many of our trips, several individuals walked barefoot.

On Wednesday, June 26, 1996, just after our lunch of bread and water…Wednesdays and Fridays were fast days, and bread and water were the only food items consumed, our group was told we could have coffee and peanut and jam on our bread, as most of us were from America and were not accustomed to fasting.

I had decided to walk up Cross Mountain, Krizevec, in Croatia, about 1,693 feet above sea level. We had been advised by our tour guide that we probably should not try to walk up the hill that day because the temperature was in the high nineties.

I said to myself, *No way I am not going. After all, I have been playing three sets of tennis several times a week in those temperatures.* I did make the climb, praying my Rosary along the way. I had a picture taken in front of the Cross and found a soft rock to sit on (see image) After praying another Rosary, I made my climb down the hill and got back to the house around 3:00 pm. As soon as I arrived, Tom, one of the group who was there with his wife and daughter, beckoned for me to join him and his family. They were looking up at the sky, and he said to me, "Tom, look at the Sun!"

I did, and to my amazement, the Sun appeared as a large white bread wafer, spinning around. At the same time, I saw a large, bright Cross. I had an orange soda and some chips in my hands and sat down and watched these phenomena for several minutes while eating the chips and drinking the soda. I had read about these phenomena happening to others, but now they were happening to me!

That same night, a Wednesday, our group had walked up Apparition Hill, awaiting Ivan and some of the other young people (Seers) to whom the Virgin Mary was appearing, and giving her message for all of us. The apparitions usually occurred between 10:00 and 10:30 pm, and our group had settled in place on any rock we could find, several hours earlier. There was a beautiful sunset, and while watching, I saw the Sun go behind some clouds, and then I saw three Suns appear from behind the clouds.

I said to myself, *This represents the Trinity; the Father, Son, and Holy Spirit.*

The next night, Thursday, I had one more surprise, one more blessing. Several of our group shared that as we were leaving Apparition Hill, we had seen the Cross on Cross Mountain as fiery red or a large orange ball of fire with a Rosary surrounding it.

Since returning from Medjugorje, I have had the links on two of my Rosaries turn gold on several occasions. Also, I have been able to look directly at the Sun and see it as a large white wafer, at times spinning for several minutes, without any damage to my eyes!

In August of 2005, I returned to Medjugorje with another group. On this trip, which originated in Birmingham, Alabama, with a chartered flight, I was able to hug Marjia, one of the Seers who still sees the Virgin Mary every day.

I told her about our daughter, Maria, who had been killed in an auto accident on August 19, 2003, and she gave me a big hug! (See picture of Maria). I like to think that after each trip to Medjugorje, I have returned home a better human being with an increase in the virtues of Faith, Hope, and Charity.

I continued my work at Providence and Howard, with occasional Operations at Columbia Hospital, the all-Women`s Hospital, in down town DC, now closed.

Many of the Hospitals in DC, and throughout the country, were having financial problems, some closing.

Pope Francis had visited the United States in September 2015, and visited Providence Hospital and the Emergency Room had been named after him.

I began a private practice in General Surgery in the Washington DC Metropolitan area, which I maintained until February 2003. During thirty years of practice, I became a Diplomate of the American College and was certified by the American Board of Surgery in November 1971; I also became a fellow of the American College of Surgery on October 18, 1973.

Other achievements included becoming a life member of the American Medical Tennis Association, US Tennis Association, and American Society of Abdominal Surgeons (January 1975); a Fellow of the American College of Nutrition (1992); and now Emeritus of the College of Nutrition, Emeritus Clinical Associate Professor of Surgery at Howard University, Emeritus member of the National Medical Association, and lifetime member of the American College of Surgery.

Tennis Family of the Year

A memorable event took place on November 11, 1993. The Thomas Calhoun family received the Family of the Year Award from the US Tennis Association, Mid-Atlantic Section. (See copy of award.)

Shirley and I teamed in mixed doubles for two tournaments. The first was the Washington Area Tennis Patrons Tournament in the 1970s, a charity event, which we won. The tournament is no longer held.

The final time was in the ATA Nationals in Boston, Massachusetts, in August 1973where we lost in the finals of the mixed doubles to Tyrone Mapp and Ann Koger.

Visit to China and Japan

Shirley and I were members of the Visiting Physicians, Spouses, and District of Columbia Medical Leaders who traveled to Japan and China in November 1980.

This was a memorable event. We visited the People's Republic of China and Japan from November 15, 1980, through December 4, 1980.

This was the first time Westerners were allowed into the country since 1949 when the civil war ended and Mao Zedong, the Communist rebel had died.

We left Dulles International Airport at 7:30 am, landing in San Francisco at 11:27 am PST. Shirley and I stayed at her parents' house overnight and departed the next day for Tokyo Japan, arriving at 12:00 am PST. Soon we were on a Japanese Airliner headed to Hong Kong, having traveled halfway around the world in twenty-four hours. We would stay at the Hong Kong Sheraton Hotel.

The next day, we toured Hong Kong Island, Tiger Balm Garden, and Victoria Peak to name a few sights. Other sights included a Vietnamese refugee camp. Then we traveled by rail to Canton and Foshan, where we viewed an Acrobatic show. We took a plane ride to Shanghai, visited a Chemistry and Physics classroom, and then continued by boat on the Whangpoo River to the mouth of the Yangtze River.

The Physicians traveled with *the barefoot doctors* to the communes and livestock quarters. We also witnessed a major orthopedic surgical procedure, where local and acupuncture anesthesia were used, the first such application any of us from America had seen. The ladies were given tours of a Cloisonné factory, and we all visited the Terra Cotta Museum, which held a group of statues of military soldiers.

Since we were coming up on Thanksgiving, we had a lavish Thanksgiving dinner with Peking duck.

Tuesday, December 2, 1980, was Shirley's and my thirteenth wedding anniversary and the day we were scheduled to take a train to visit the Ming Tomb and the Great Wall. Shirley did not feel well that day and decided not to go, instead relaxing at the hotel. (See images of Shirley and me in Tiananmen Square in Beijing, China.)

We were back in time for dinner, Peking duck again, and thankfully, she was feeling much better and we enjoyed an evening of connubial bliss!

Before leaving for the trip, there were about three different vaccinations which all of us had. Still, everyone got sick, except Shirley, either with a cough or fever during the trip, which we had been forewarned would happen. I developed a cough and sore throat when leaving Peking, now called Beijing, as we were traveling to Narita, Japan; however, those symptoms resolved overnight.

We had to wait in the plane in Narita leaving for Los Angeles International Airport because of the frigid temperature. The plane would not start and had to be jump-started.

While we waited, suddenly, armed Japanese soldiers came on the plane and interrogated all of us but soon left, and we were allowed to take off.

Soon after we arrived back in the States, Shirley developed difficulty swallowing, and I have often wondered if it was in some way related to our trip.

Senior Surgeon, Police and Fire Department

One of the experiences I had was working as a Senior Surgeon for the Police and Fire Department here in DC. On occasions, I went with the police on sting operations. I was very much saddened by these occasions because they always involved young Black juveniles, never any other race, in some criminal pursuit … though I would have been just as sad irrespective of the ethnicity of the youngsters.

In 1981, as Clinical Associate Professor of Surgery ay Howard as I noted earlier, I was appointed Chief of Clinical Service for the newly established Integrated Surgical Residency Program at Providence Hospital, now affiliated with Howard University College of Medicine.

At Providence Hospital, I established and became the Director of the Nutritional Support Service, writing guidelines and providing leadership in the use of the newly emerging disciplines of Enteral and Parenteral Nutrition (ENT and TPN).

I also established guidelines for nutritional support services at DC General Hospital and the then open Capitol Hill Hospital, in northeast Washington DC, where I had Admitting and Operating privileges also.

First Minimally Invasive Procedure

In February 1991, I performed the first Laparoscopic Cholecystectomy (minimally invasive removal of the Gall Bladder) at Providence Hospital on a young female patient who had had a diagnosis of Acute Cholecystitis and Cholelithiasis (inflammation and gall stones)) with a successful outcome. The patient was discharged the following morning, and after a follow-up visit with me in one week, she returned to work the following day.

Concussion

Another memorable event occurred during Lent, March 1991.

I left my office around 3:30 p.m. for a dental appointment at 4:00 p.m. As I was driving down Third Street northwest, to my left, I saw this old Cadillac coming toward me, and I wondered if this guy driving was going to stop at that stop sign. The next thing I knew, there was a crash, and I was hanging upside down in my seat belt in my green Chevy van! Then I heard a lady crying and screaming at me through the open window on the driver's side.

I told her, "Lady, you have to calm down ... and please call my wife, Shirley, and tell her I have been in an accident." I gave her the phone number.

The next thing I remember were voices saying, "Cut him out! Cut him out!" Then I heard voices saying, "Get him in for a CAT scan!"

I had been taken to the Washington Hospital Center (WHC).

Shirley told me I called her seven times that night asking her to call the dentist and cancel my appointment and to call the office of Dr. Warren Strudwick (now deceased), whom I was covering for, as he was out of town, and tell them I was in an accident.

When it was related to me later, I had been *T-boned* by a man in an old Cadillac who ran a stop sign, and I had sustained a concussion.

The Cadillac was the vertical beam of the T and my van, the horizontal beam.

I was discharged home in three days, improved, having required only conservative measures.

One of the first things I remember when I arrived home was hearing Maria come into my room and ask, "Hi, Stitch, how are you doing?"

Sometime later, I had the thought that I would write about this experience and title it "Stitch."

I never have. Before I could return to work, I had to have a neuropsychological clearance.

After a successful clearance, it happened that there was a three-day course in Indianapolis, Indiana, on minimally invasive surgery techniques.

I took the course because I wanted to be sure that I could continue operating using these techniques, which require special hand-to-eye coordination. I resumed my usual work schedule in about a month. There was a residual effect that I noted for several months after the event. When backing out of my driveway and looking over my left shoulder, I had a bit of discomfort; also when I resumed playing tennis, I noted some definite discomfort when I tossed my ball up to serve.

Catholic Archdiocese Health-Care Network

As one of the original members of the Catholic Archdiocese Health-Care Network established in the mid-1980s, I was privileged to be able to provide pro bono surgical services at Providence Hospital for over thirty years for District metropolitan residents.

From April 4, 2018, until June 30, 2020, I worked part-time for Catholic Charities here in DC, helping revise some outdated policies in emergency preparedness and quality improvement.

I was appointed to the Commission on Healing Arts and Licensure (now DC Board of Medicine) by Mayor Marion Berry and was elected Vice President in 1984.

Recognition, Awards

I received the John Carroll Society Health-Care Award for Outstanding Community Service in March 25, 2001, and the District of Columbia Medical Society's (DCMS) Physicians' Distinguished Service Award in November. At that time, I wrote "The Surgeon's Prayer," which was approved for printing "with ecclesiastical approval" by Reverend Isidore Dixon, the censor deputatus, from the Archdiocese of Washington DC. (See "The Surgeon's Prayer".)

I became a member of the National Capitol Reciprocal Insurance Company (NCRIC), the organization that provided liability insurance to physicians in the District of Columbia in 1980. I was elected secretary of the board of governors of NCRIC and the secretary to the executive committee, a salaried position in 1982, which I held until my retirement for the practice of surgery in 2003. Following retirement from the practice of surgery, I worked as the first medical director for the Emergency Health and Medical Services Administration, a division of the DC Department of Health. Two major health issues the District experienced were Lead in the water, leeching from fifty-year-old lead pipes and a toxic Mercury spill at two public schools in southeast Washington, both of which had the potential for long-term illnesses. After several months of mitigation, these issues were resolved with no known recorded morbidity or mortality.

I had a number of interesting, to me, experiences as Medical Director for EHMSA.

One consisted of getting vaccinated for smallpox. America was just at the start of the conflict with Iraq, so a number of individuals had to be vaccinated, including many of those working in the State Department who were deploying to Iraq.

Anthrax in DC

Another major event that affected the entire country was the anthrax attack in which several people died, including two men at the main post office here in DC. I helped provide prophylactic antibiotics to over thirty thousand individuals who were thought to have been infected by anthrax.

Following these events and working with Dr. Daniel Lucey, the Medical Director for the DC Department of Health at the time, I enrolled in graduate school and received a Master of Science degree in Biohazardous Threat Agents and Emerging Infectious Diseases from Georgetown University here in Washington DC in May 2007.

Currently, I am an Emeritus Clinical Associate Professor of Surgery at Howard University Department of Surgery in Washington DC. From the time we moved to 4010 until December 2015 when we sold the house, we lived, worked, and prayed at this domicile.

Pilgrimage to Rome

In 2006, Shirley decided she wanted to go to Rome, so we made arrangements for her to go with a group headed by Cardinal Theodore McCarrick. Upon returning, she related how exciting the trip was. She visited the Sistine Chapel and viewed Michelangelo's work *The Creation of Adam*, *The Flood*, and *The Last Judgment*, just to mention a few of the sights. The Catholic world was upended some years later when numerous sexual scandals were reported in the Catholic church. Cardinal Theodore McCarrick, who was archbishop for Washington DC for over ten years, was found to have been involved with insalubrious behavior characteristic of those scandals.

He was laicized, dismissed from the clergy, by Pope Francis on February 16, 2016, although he remained a priest.[11]

In 2013, Pope Francis had decreed that Pope John Paul II and Pope John XXIII were to be canonized on Divine Mercy Sunday, April 27, 2014, and become saints.

I had decided I was going to Rome for the canonization, and after Shirley and I discussed it, I made arrangements to join a group sponsored by the *Catholic Standard* magazine, a popular metropolitan Catholic magazine.

I departed from 4010 Argyle Terrace on a mid-April afternoon in a Blue Van for the trip to Dulles International Airport in Virginia from which we would leave for Rome. Our Catholic faith teaches us that the evil one, Satan, is always trying to create problems, so I was not overly upset with the events that transpired.

Our van was passing through Ward Circle near American University in northwest DC, a very busy area, in the afternoon. I had a seat near a window and witnessed a young lady plow into the van, just below where I was sitting. Fortunately, all of the cars were driving at a rate of ten miles per hour or less. No one was injured, nor was there any significant damage done to either vehicle.

Our van driver was visibly upset and stopped the van in the spot where it was hit. Very soon thereafter, a policeman arrived and had him move the van to the side. I told the driver that I saw the entire incident and gave him my name and address. He had to contact his home office, and this action stretched into more than an hour.

About this time, those of us who needed to be on time for our flight became more and more anxious. Thankfully, another Blue Van did arrive, and we were able to reach the airport in time for our flight.

I had not yet met my roommate but did so at the airport, although we had talked via phone previously. He told me he had called my home and talked with Shirley to see if I was coming, and I told him about the accident.

The flight to Rome was uneventful, but to me, it was a blessing in the making. We checked into the Crowne Plaza Hotel, which I noted had two red clay tennis courts, and I wished I had brought my tennis rackets.

---

[11] www.americanmagazine.org>faith>2019/02>form.

My left hip was becoming more and more painful, and I began wondering if I would need surgery again, having had the left hip implant surgery in April 2011.

Our tour guide met us at the airport, and after receiving our agenda for the week, we had dinner and retired for the evening.

On Divine Mercy Sunday, April 27, 2014, our wake-up call at the hotel was 3:00 a.m. After a hot breakfast of eggs, bacon, sausage, fruit, milk, juice, and coffee or tea, we boarded our bus at 4:00 am. It would take us to the drop-off spot along Gregory VII Road, from which we walked to St. Peter's Square.

The estimates for the crowd for the dual canonizations were in the millions, so our guide had prepared us for an early start in order to get a good viewing space for the Mass and canonization. Mass was scheduled to begin at 10:30 a.m., and we reached St. Peter's Square about 5:30 am.

In addition to analgesics, pain-killing medications, my medications included a diuretic, a water pill, as treatment for my high blood pressure, which generally requires visiting a bathroom several times a day.

One of my main prayers that day was that I could control my need to urinate. There were bathroom facilities throughout the square, but with some 900,000 people present by 10:00 am, movement was almost impossible.

Thankfully, that prayer was answered, and I was able to stand for over eleven hours by the time I had walked back to the Hotel and never had the urge to urinate.

A young lady did offer me her stool during the events, and I did sit for about five minutes, which did refresh me. I was able to receive Communion from one of the hundreds of priests available, who insisted I receive it on my tongue and not in my hands.

After the services, which lasted several hours, I tried to flag a cab down for the trip back to the hotel, not realizing that one had to go to the cab stand to get a cab, unlike in America, where one could hail a cab by a hand wave.

There was a light rain falling during my walk back to the hotel, so from time to time, I stopped at some of the shops, not having to enter.

The next day there was a trip to the Catacombs and the Sistine Chapel, where we viewed Michelangelo's works, among many others.

We also took a trip to Umbria and made a visit to the Assisi, where St. Francis lived.

Of the many eye-catching works of Michelangelo were *The Creation* and *The Last Judgment*. One of my favorites was the *Pietà*. The *Pietà* is a statue of The Virgin Mary holding the body of her dead son, Jesus, on her lap. The statue seems to have been made from a creamy, white marble on a slightly gray background. The white color portrays purity, and the gray, to me, represents a strong, silent picture of accepted suffering.

A thick glass shields the *Pietà* from hands anxious to touch it. Other striking views were the *Transfiguration* by Raphael, the painting of Saint Helen, mother of Emperor Constantine, who brought the cross and nails of Christ's crucifixion to Rome by Bernini, and the one of Saint Jerome, who transcribed the Bible from Greek to Latin by Leonardo da Vinci, to name a few, all of which were painted centuries earlier.

We were able to see Pope Francis as he drove about the square before the day was over.

Pope Francis visited DC in 2015. He canonized St. Junipera Serra at the Basilica of the National Shrine of the Immaculate Conception, the first such event America.[12]

In 1979, Pope John Paul II, now St. John Paul II, came to DC, and I took Tom Jr., Christine, and Kathy to see him at Haines Pont here in DC. Maria was only four years old, and she stayed home with Shirley.

In 2008, as a member of the John Carroll's Society, I was blessed with being an Usher on the grounds of the Washington baseball stadium when Pope Benedict XVI came to DC.

Annual Physical Exam

After my annual physical exam, which included a digital rectal exam (DRE) by my Urologist, Dr. Alex Fangonil (who has given permission to use his name) and review of my prostate-specific antigen (PSA), he called and asked if Shirley and I would come to his office.

When a Doctor asks for the patient and spouse to come to the office, something significant is going on. A week earlier, I had had an X-ray-guided

---

[12] www.washingtonpost.com>acys>of.faith.2015/09/23.

biopsy of my prostate by Alex so I was pretty sure we had to discuss prostate cancer. The main function of the prostate is to secrete fluid, one of the components of semen, as well as PSA, which is a tumor marker, valuable as a screening test for prostate cancer.

"Only mammals have Prostate Glands and Breasts. Countries which have high rates of Breast Cancer have high rates of Prostate Cancer, and countries which have low rates of Prostate cancer have relatively low rates of Breast Cancer."[13]

A value of less than 4.0 nanograms per milliliter (ng/ml) is considered normal, and my values had been increasing over the past few years from 0.5 to 4.0. With a suspicious DRE findings, we had elected to have a biopsy. This normal value of the PSA is not recognized as absolute by some physicians.

We discussed a treatment plan, based on my clinical condition. (I was in great shape, and in fact, I had entered an upcoming men's seventy singles tennis tournament.)

We discussed the treatment options; watchful waiting, doing nothing, brachytherapy (i.e., implantation of radiation seeds within the prostate) and external beam radiation therapy (EBRT) for a prescribed length of time as an outpatient, or surgery.

My pathology report indicated that I had adenocarcinoma of the prostate, low grade, stage 1, Gleasons 5. This system of grading was devised during the years 1960 and 1970 by Dr. Donald Gleason, a Pathologist in Minnesota. We agreed that I would have EBRT, and after consultation with an Oncologist (cancer specialist), a period of forty-three days was recommended.

I completed forty-three days of treatment on April 27, 2005.

I have the copyright for the title, *Forty-Three Days: A Surgeon's Wake-Up Call*, a book that describes my activities, the agony and the ecstasy, during those forty-three days.

I did enter the tennis tournament and won my first round six to three, six to three, but lost the next round by the same score. Would I have done

---

[13] hopkinsmedicine.org/brady-urology-institute/specialities/condition-and-treatments/Prostate-Cancer/prostate-cancer-questions/exploring-the-link-between-evolution-and-prostate.

better in the tournament if I did not have to deal with the cancer? Who knows?

After about seven or eight days, I began to experience one of the common expected side effects of the radiation—increased urinary frequency. Because I had to go to the bathroom frequently, I slept in the room I used for my office, so as not to awake Shirley. Thankfully, this subsided after about three weeks. I drank many bottles of Gatorade, but I was not at full strength for a tennis tournament.

As of this writing, no single cause of prostate cancer has been identified but research does indicate that diet plays a vital role in the development of prostate cancer. (See previous footnote also.)

As for me now, sixteen and a half years after completing radiation therapy and one treatment with Lupron (Lp) in June 2017, I am doing well with no active signs of cancer.

I do not know what my current PSA is, but at age eighty-eight, why should I know…because I have decided on no further treatment, except pain control if indicated, None of us lives forever![14]

Lupron (leuprolide acetate) is a synthetic, gonadotropin-releasing hormone treatment that reduces levels of testosterone in men and treats endometriosis in women.

In February 2003, I had made the decision to stop my active practice of surgery. I came to this decision after many discussions with Shirley, bolstered by my discussion with a spiritual advisor at a Catholic retreat. He advised that if I was going to accept a position I had been offered as a medical director in the DC Department of Health, I should do it on a full-time basis and devote all my time and energies to it.

After the anthrax event in DC, where two men in the main post office died from the infection in October 2001, there was another scare in March 2002 for which prophylactic antibiotics were administered. Then in February 2003, the same time I had begun full-time work as a Medical Director in the DC Department of Health, there was a mini crisis of Lead contamination of potable water in the District of Columbia. After multiple investigations, it was determined that this was due to fifty-year-old lead pipes in DC, which were leaching Lead, resulting in bottled water being distributed to the residents while the problem was corrected.

---

[14] https://www.rxlist.com>lupron-side-effects-drug-center.

By September, over eight hundred residents with ages ranging from six months to ninety years old had their blood drawn for Lead levels.

Five to fourteen micrograms per deciliter (µg/dl) is noted as a normal range; however, for children, any value over five should warrant medical attention.[15] In adults, up to 10 µg/dl is considered safe, but values greater than 10 should be evaluated by a physician.

Following these events, I decided to enter the graduate program at Georgetown University here in DC, and in May 2007, I received the Master of Science degree in Biohazardous Threat Agents and Emerging Infectious Diseases.

There was a toxic Mercury spill at a local High School in October 2003 as noted above which we addressed.

I have cancer of the prostate, as did Jenk, the disease from which he expired; however, I was fortunate in having an early diagnosis and stage 1 disease.

Jenk and I knew the ATA Nationals would be held in Baltimore, Maryland, on August 3, 2017, the 100 year Anniversary of the ATA, and we were planning to go and enter the men's 80 doubles.

We had no doubt that there were no eighty-year-old dudes who were going to beat us!

We lost to Leon Bowser and Walter Moore, 5-7. 0-6, as I previously noted, and we were the only two teams entered.

Of our many reflections about tennis, he recalled his four years of playing on the tennis team at Saint Louis University in Saint Louis, Missouri. During that time, he noted, he lost only three singles matches, and in 1961, he won the Missouri Valley Conference Championship. (See images.)

We had many discussions about Prostate Cancer, and I often told him that the disease differed in individuals depending on the stage it was first diagnosed.

We talked about several of our male tennis-playing friends having had prostate cancer, several having expired, though I did not mention the deaths to him when we talked.

---

[15] health.ny.gov/publications/2526.pdf; medlineplus.gov>Medical Encyclopedia.

We spoke on several occasions within the last two years, twice face to face when I visited him at the hospital and nursing home in which he lived in Richmond, Virginia.

I was blessed in that his daughter, Kimberly, allowed us to talk briefly a few days before he peacefully expired.

So as of now, we are in the midst of a pandemic, caused by the COVID-19 coronavirus, for which there are several vaccines.

A pandemic is a disease prevalent all over the world.

The pandemic has resulted in visits to nursing homes, including Carroll Manor here in the District of Columbia, in which Shirley is a resident, being curtailed.

Visitation restrictions have been relaxed since all the staff and residents at most nursing homes in the country have been vaccinated.

There were four deaths in Carroll Manor, where Shirley is, and she has been moved to a separate COVID-free floor.

We have had several face-to-face visits in the last several months.

So now my rhetorical question to the two of us Black Hawks now living, me and Furman, is "What's next?"

CHAPTER 12
REFLECTIONS

In November 2007, I went to Jacksonville on a business trip. One of the first persons I contacted was Alvin White whom I mentioned earlier. The first night, Alvin had contacted several of our friends, members of the Black Hawks—Henry, Oscar, and Furman—and we all met at Alvin's home for a great steak dinner and conversation about old times.

On my last night in town, Alvin, Jamie, and I had a great dinner at Red Lobster, and just seeing some of my old friends was most comforting.

On one of the many phone calls Jenk and I had, we discussed writing our memoirs. The plan was for the Black Hawks who were alive at the time—Henry, Furman, Jenk, and me—to write our recollections of our time and activities since the end of the Hawks.

Earl Thomas Cullins had died some years earlier from Parkinson's Disease, and we were unable to make any contact with Paschal Collins. Oscar Fletcher

Oscar died from colon cancer in 2016.

I called Henry and Furman, who are still living in Jacksonville on several occasions and told them of Jenk's and my plan to write our memoirs.

They were eager to go forward with the project at the time and agreed to send me their information, however they never did.

In November 2014, I obtained the copyright for the title of the book, *The Last of the Black Hawks: Memoirs of Childhood Friends*, by Thomas Calhoun, MD, and Wilbur H. Jenkins Jr., Esq.

I reached out again in 2019 to Furman, and he did give me some information, which is included, and he sent me a copy of the City Basketball

Championship Award, which is a part of the Book Cover. The award is for the year 1951, however, the Black Hawks won the title in 1948, and there was no award made.

Henry died in the spring of this year, 2021, from complications of prostate cancer.

Jenk sent some information and much of his recollections were being transcribed by a friend in Richmond, Virginia, where he was living at the time. They are included.

Because of a series of strokes, Jenk was unable to recall much of his early background so I have recorded for both of us what I recall.

During most of his time in the Air Force, Jenk was based in Germany.

There were several events in DC during the fall and winter of 1958 of note, we agreed.

We were staying in the basement with Mrs. Freeman at 3005 Eleventh Street NW as I have previously noted. At some point, we played against an up-and-coming young Colored junior team, brothers named Henry and Randall Kennedy. Henry would become a judge in Washington DC and Randall a professor of law at Harvard and the author of a somewhat controversial book titled *Nigger*.

At this time also, Edgemoor Country Club in Bethesda, Maryland, a suburb of DC, had allowed a number of Colored players to play in a tennis tournament at the Club for the first time.

I gained a bit of recognition in that I upset one of the White seeded players, 6-4, 6-4 four, in the first round but lost in the next round to a higher seed.

Jenk and I lost to the number-one seeded doubles team, the Dell brothers, whom we had to play in the first round.

Some years later, Norm Fitz, about whom more will be said later, became the first Black male accepted as a member of the Edgemoor Club.

Harold Freeman also told me that years earlier he had been invited as the first Colored tennis players to play in a tournament being held at Edgemoor.

One of the brothers, Donald, would become an Attorney and close friend of Arthur Ashe and Jenk.

After the Nationals in 1958 in DC, a potentially dangerous racial incident involving Jenk and me occurred one afternoon as we were escorting two young White girls to the campus of Howard University. The four of us were awaiting the traffic light to change for us to cross the street when I turned to look behind us. There was this White guy with a four-by-four poised to hit one of us. About the same time, Jenk turned around, and we stared the guy down. He left.

During his time in Law school at Howard, Jenk teamed up with Norman Fitz, who would become a lifelong friend of Jenk's and mine. Some years later, they won the men's doubles title, beating the Freeman brothers in the Mall tournament (see picture).

Norm would forge his own odyssey in tennis, being ranked as a top player in DC, the mid-Atlantic area, and the nation. Further, in 1980, he was one of only two Black umpires to go to the Wimbledon Championships in London, England.

In the men's singles, age 70 category, Norm was ranked in the top five in the nation.

Norm and I also played with each other in doubles and against each other for many years in DC.

Our singles matches were always tough, and unfortunately for me, he won most of them. The good thing is we always could have a beer after the matches and have maintained our friendship.

A quote from a letter I received from him on August 2, 2020, follows: "I just want you to know what an influence our relationship with Jenk has meant to me. Without you and Jenk setting the standards with your impeccable character and sportsmanship, along with so many others, I would never have chosen this path. Your friend for life, Norman." (See pictures of Norm and Jenk and the Freeman brothers, Clyde and Harold, both physicians.)

Norm and I won the men's 35 ATA doubles title in Boston in 1972, and he won the men's 35 singles title then and again in 1974 in DC.

There were numerous incidents and adventures Jenk and I shared over the years, much of which I believe he would have noted had he lived longer.

A note, Christmas card from him, and picture of him with Arthur Ashe's wife are included.

I was quite pleasantly surprised by the tribute he wrote to Arthur Ashe, "In Memoriam," by Wilbur Jenkins, Lifelong Friend, a copy of which he sent me and I included.

Jenk and I played numerous doubles tournaments during the past years and were finalists in the ATA's National men's 70 doubles, played in Richmond, Virginia, in 2003.

In September 2003, he, Doris, and Kimberly visited with us here in DC after Maria's untimely death, her having been struck by a hit-and-run eighteen-wheeler truck on August 19, 2003 (See picture of Maria.)

He noted that it was while in Law School at Howard University that he reconnected with Doris Sroufe and her sister, Frances, whom we had met some years earlier at a party.

We discussed some of his experiences working with Clarence Thomas at the Equal Employment Opportunity Agency, before he, Attorney Thomas, became a member of the Supreme Court.

During this time, we also discussed some of his experiences in St. Louis, where he had a tennis scholarship, which covered 60 percent of his tuition and the GI Bill the remainder, the latter I also used to help when I was in medical school.

Of our many reflections about tennis, he recalled his four years of playing on the tennis team at Saint Louis University in Saint Louis, Missouri. During that time, he noted he lost only three singles matches and in 1961 won the Missouri Valley Conference Championship. (See newspaper clipping and photographs.)

Jenk's wife, Doris, a registered nurse, called me when his weight zoomed to 230 plus pounds. He was taking various nutritional supplements, and she told me his liver enzymes, according to blood tests that reflect the status of one's liver, were abnormal. I advised him that I thought these various supplements in the amounts he was taking were likely affecting his health. He accepted my advice and eliminated most of these supplements, and with changes in his diet, over several months, he did lose much of the weight.

When Doris became ill during the months before she died, the three of us talked often via phone about her health and tests she should have. I have always felt honored they respected my medical opinions about issues we discussed.

Unfortunately, I could not attend Doris's funeral, as I was in the process of having the first of my three hip replacement procedures.

Even in the past few years, Jenk often called me to discuss some of his medical issues and on occasions to advise him against some medications he wanted to take.

Jenk expired on July 7, this year, 2020, from metastatic prostate cancer.

The year 2020 was unlike any other in my lifetime.

When the pandemic with the COVID-19 virus started, my part-time job at Catholic Charities was not renewed because of lack of funds, brought on by the pandemic. Shirley had her seventy-seventh birthday. I had my eighty-eighth birthday on October 6. Joseph Biden was elected the second Catholic president of the United States.

Interestingly, for Catholics, Pope Francis indicated this was "the year of Saint Joseph."

The Capitol and Congressional Buildings were invaded by a group of President Trump's sympathizers on January 6, with resulting deaths and ongoing non-intended consequences.

Jamie, my lifelong friend from Jacksonville, told me he was diagnosed with the COVID infection, and later, after several weeks of hospitalization and time in a rehabilitation facility, he was finally improved and back home.

As of this writing, he has not received his first COVID vaccination.

Shirley and all of the nursing home residents and staff have received two injections, and some visiting restrictions may soon be lifted.

I received my second shot at 11:55 a.m. on February 17, 2021, and by 7:00 p.m., I had trouble raising my left shoulder, the arm of my vaccination. Because of the pain, I took an extra-strength Tylenol. The next morning, I had trouble getting out of bed. I had flulike symptoms, fatigue, and generalized body aches, so I took another Tylenol and went back to bed.

As the day progressed, I was better, and on the second day, I was back to normal.

As of this writing, hundreds of thousands of Americans have become infected and died from the COVID infection.

Further, there is now the delta variant, considered to be more infectious than the original virus. It is now infecting many individuals under age sixty-five.

There are several vaccines available now with efficacy rates of over 90 percent, and whereas millions of Americans are vaccinated, a large number have refused to be vaccinated.

At some future d ate, someone is going to write a book about COVID-19, perhaps similar to "*The Great Influenza*" by John M. Barry about the disease in 1917–1918, and it will become a best seller for those alive to read it.

My final thoughts are now there are only two Black Hawks living, Furman and me.

Also dying from prostate cancer were Drs. Aaron Jackson and Oswald Warner and another close friend of Jenk's and mine, a tennis player, Paul Alexander.

Two other tennis buddies, Dr. Clyde Freeman and Jim Ridgley, also died from prostate cancer.

At this point, my prostate cancer appears to be dormant or stable.

Jamie also has prostate cancer and was treated with implanted Radium Seeds within the prostate "over ten years ago he states" and when last we talked over the phone, all w could say is "we are blessed".

The SURGEON`S PRAYER

O Lord, you have given me the grace, the privilege, the responsibility, to be your servant. Indeed, you have given all mankind this gift, but to me especially, the gift of being a Surgeon.

You have prepared me Lord, to be able to sustain the long hours of study and training for this special service, to be the instrument through which you bring healing and comfort, and at times, as it pleases you, cure.

Thank you Lord for this grace, this vocation, and please grant that I may know always that it is you who are the Source, and to you goes the glory!

To be able to lay on our fellowman the cold blade of the steel scalpel or the heat of the cautery, without fear or timidity, and remove diseased flesh, created by you, does not come from man, but surely the promptings of the Holy Spirit.

I beg you Lord, keep me humble, for you know me through and through. Do not permit the Tempter to cloud my mind and make me doubt your mercies, but grant me to know and accept that though my hands are the instruments, it is you who are in control.

Please give me the grace to be patient with my patients, to give them the time and comfort, and at times, of just being there and listening.

If you bless me with a spouse and family, please give me the love and time for them and they for me, for you know the demands of your servant, the Surgeon.

Help me to know also Lord, when not to operate, wisdom that can come only from you.

Let this wisdom guide me also Lord, to be able to know and accept that day when it is time to stop being a Surgeon, and just be your faithful servant, for however long you may so desire.

Thomas Calhoun MD, MS, FACS.

Shirley Calhoun at Tianamen Square in Beijing, China, November 1985.

Tom Calhoun in Tianamen Square, Beijing, China, November 1985 (TS)

Tom Calhoun in front of Cross on Cross Mountain
in Medjugorje, Yugoslavia (Mej.com)

Blue Cross in Medjugorje

Tom Calhoun in Blue Cap on Apparition Hill in Medjugorje
in June, 1996. I do not know the names or where abouts of
the other people so you can remove them if necessary)

Tom Calhoun receiving the National Intercollegiate Singles Tennis
Trophy as Winner for Historically Black Colleges and Universities
from Coach Walt Austin, in pants (now deceased)

Tom and Shirley in New Orleans, La.

CIA Headquarters in Langley, Virginia; Calhoun in pink shirt on the right end, with Graduate Class from Georgetown University in DC.

Sylviua (Syl) Thompson, biological Mother of Tom Calhoun

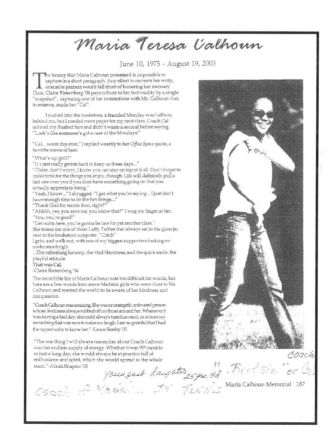

Maria Calhoun (deceased) youngest Daughter of Tom and Shirley.

Shirley Jones, before her marriage to Tom Calhoun

Award to The Black Hawks Basketball Team.
(Winners in 1948, Award give in 1951).

Will Jenkins Jr., at a Tennis Match while at St. Louis University.

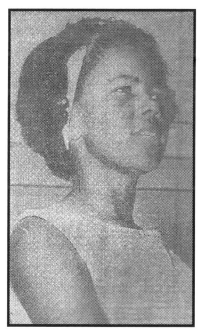

Shirley Jones before marriage to Tom Calhoun; show Image
only, omit writing, I do not know where it is

Wil the third and Kimberly, adult
children of Wil and Doris Jenkins.

Tom and Shirley with
their children

Will on his Obituary

The time came at the age of 32

Rated the world's No. 1 as they were convinced to do;

Previously he married Jeanne a talented artist in her own right.

Expert with a camera; in and out of sight.

She had already published a book;

Beautiful enough to model with a unique look

and then came Camera and they were three;

a marvelous family for all to see.

I loved him beyond words.

He set his bar quite high.

His fans admired him as he lit up the sky.

We may never see his like again;

God welcomed him home as his life came to an end.

Sincerely,

Wilbur Jenkins Jr.

Wil and Arthur Ashe (now deceased).

Will Jenkins, A student at St. Louis University

Adult children of Tom and Shirley Calhoun, Kathy and
Tom Jr., top, Christine and Maria, bottom

Calhoun as a teenager

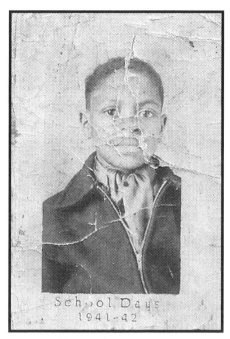

Tom Calhoun as age 9

Mid Atlantic Award for Calhoun family

Drs. Clyde and Harold Freeman in white tennis attire, from left to right, finalists in Mall Tennis Club Tennis tournament, Washington, DC

Graduation from Medical School on June 10, 1963

CHAPTER 13
WILBUR HAMPTON (JENK) JENKINS JR.

I, Wilbur Hampton Jenkins Jr., was born in Jacksonville, Florida, to Mr. and Mrs. Wilbur Jenkins Sr. Their union lasted four and one-half years, beginning in 1932. Eleven years later, my mother became Mrs. Gertrude Teasley, the wife of a World War II veteran named Pate Teasley. He and my father fought in World War II, and sometimes they were as close as thirty miles to each other when they were in Europe.

Growing up, I attended Saint Pius Catholic Elementary School for Negroes. The Priests and Nuns were excellent teachers. On Sunday mornings, my great-grandmother would take me to a primitive Baptist church, where the members were known to fall out and speak in tongues anytime during the service. From Monday to Friday, I learned Latin, and my religious training was dramatically diverse.

I attended Stanton High School, which was a public educational institution. With a November birthday, along with combining my sixth- and seventh-grade classes, I was able to graduate at the age of sixteen in 1950. While I was in school, I became a newsboy for the *Jacksonville Journal*. I won numerous contests with subscriptions and received gifts such as trips to Washington DC, New York City, and Havana, Cuba! While on these trips, I was accompanied by two young men who later became surgeons, Dr. Earl Thomas Cullins and Dr. Thomas Calhoun. I also became a newsboy for the *Florida Times Union*, and as I aged, I subsequently delivered telegrams.

Before I attended Florida A&M College, I participated in basketball at the LaVilla playground, and I was elected captain of the Black Hawks. Some of my teammates were Henry Rhim, who went on to become a reverend; Furman Adams, who became a postal worker; Pascal Collins, who became a teacher, and Earl Thomas Cullins and Thomas Calhoun, both of whom became Surgeons. We won the championship our second year for the group 18 and younger. I set a record for scoring, which lasted seventeen years, and after that, I stopped checking!

After entering FAMC, I received a partial tennis scholarship. As a freshman, I competed against Ed Whitley, Charlie Weir, Henry Singletary, Paul Bowie, and Thomas Calhoun. Later, at Tuskegee, Alabama, we attended the Southern Collegiate Tennis Championships. We won our singles and doubles matches. Thomas Calhoun and I were the number-three team.

I was active in the YMCA and eventually received an award for being an outstanding member. I pledged Alpha Phi Alpha following Thomas Calhoun, but I later dropped out after finding the hazing unwelcoming. After five semesters, I dropped out and joined the US Air Force on the advice of Paschal Collins, one of the original Black Hawks.

I was assigned to basic training at Lackland Air Force Base, Texas. I was one of six Floridians from Jacksonville, Florida. I was promoted to assistant flight leader because of my leadership skills. As a young Black American, I found it to be an experience leading young White males who had only interacted with people of color as servants.

I was lucky to make friends because some members of the flight decided to give me a blanket shower. A quiet, red-headed Floridian told me when the scuttlebutt reached him, "Don't worry; me and the other Floridians and the other two Black guys are with you." This was one of several unexpected interventions in my life.

I left Lackland after being assigned to Warren Air Force Base outside of Cheyenne, Wyoming. It was there that I discovered snow for the first time. After a period of time, I was promoted to the flight leader for a flight. We had class from 6:00 a.m. to 12:00 p.m. Monday through Friday. I served in Germany and France after leaving Cheyenne. I represented the US Air Force Europe tennis team. I was the only enlisted man and only minority.

After an Honorable Discharge as a second class airman, I attended St. Louis University on a tennis scholarship. I had a record-winning nine out of ten matches, including some championships. I was elected Captain of the tennis team. Later, I was admitted to the Hall of Fame for my tennis accomplishments. (See images.)

I also graduated with a Bachelor of Science in Psychology.

While at St. Louis University, I had the pleasure of swapping aces and volleys with a high school senior named Arthur Ashe. I had met Arthur earlier on the summer American Tennis Association (ATA) tour.

The ATA was *the* tennis circuit for Blacks.

After graduation, I left St. Louis, Missouri, for Washington DC. I obtained employment as a substitute teacher and a mail clerk simultaneously.

I was accepted into Howard Law School in Washington, DC, and later graduated with a Juris Doctorate Law degree in January 1968.

I was hired as a research assistant at the US Civil Rights Commission. While there, I became aware of racial discrimination in the Middle Atlantic Tennis Association. Blacks were not allowed at some Clubs. I spoke to Arthur Ashe about this fact. He had stayed with Edgar Lee, an excellent Black senior. We resolved to do something about racism.

I wrote a letter on the commission letterhead to the US Lawn Tennis Association (USLTA), questioning this exclusionary policy; I signed my name as a research assistant. Later, Arthur Ashe went to New York City and confronted Robert Kelleher, the USLTA president. Arthur stated that he would call a national press conference within twenty-four hours if the policy was not changed.

Mr. Kelleher was startled because Arthur was known for his mild manner. He consulted Attorney Donald Dell, who was also in attendance at my wedding. Donald put his arm on Mr. Keller's shoulder and consoled him. He then asked, "You don't support that policy, do you?"

Within twenty-four hours, the policy was changed!

Arthur had shared with Donald Dell his plans to attack the policy. Donald Dell later became his attorney.

After leaving the US Civil Rights Commission, I was hired as a research assistant for the Kerner Commission on Civil Disorders. I was interviewed by an ex-CIA officer. I don't believe there is any such thing as an ex-CIA officer.

I had worked as a volunteer for SNCC and had demonstrated with the Congress of Racial Equality (CORE) in St. Louis, Missouri. Shortly thereafter, a Public Accommodation Law was passed.

My major in Law School was focused on civil rights. Most of my instructors were affiliated in some fashion with Thurgood Marshall, the first Black Supreme Court justice. He had worked with others on *Brown v. Board of Education*, the decision that declared segregated schools illegal and unconstitutional!

I minored in International Studies. I was fascinated by South Africa and the struggle with Apartheid.

I graduated in 1968 in the midyear class. Before I graduated, I had married an Ohio native, Doris Ann Sroufe. She was a registered nurse and acquainted with my best friend, Dr. Thomas Calhoun. Wilbur III was born March 1967, and Kimberly Jeneece Jenkins was born in June of 1970. We lived in southwest Washington DC. After a year, we moved to Suitland, Maryland.

I was working with the Neighborhood Legal Services Organization while Doris was employed in southern Maryland. Our first house had a basement with a bedroom and three bedrooms upstairs.

The National Association for the Advancement of Colored People (NAACP) representatives approached me to apply for a position as executive secretary for the Prince George's County Human Relations Committee. The position offered a raise and a chance to draft enabling documents for a Human Relations Commission.

I was successful in my efforts. We acquired five investigator mediators and a legal program emphasizing police-community relations. The *Washington Post* and other news media took note because Contract Definition InstructionCD1, the new law, had subpoena and cease and desist power! Some national entities had no such power.

I rejected the advice of close friends and was lucky enough to get the bill passed despite the subpoena and cease and desist legal components. I received a plaque for outstanding performance but was denied a promised raise. After three years, I left for a $6,000 raise. It was for the Health Education and Welfare Administration (HEW) as an Equal Employment Opportunity specialist.

I later worked for the Food and Drug Administration (FDA). I was requested to draw up an affirmative action plan. My plan had 50 percent of the previous plan's goal; however, my plan was rejected as being too ambitious.

The affirmative action plans had goals and timetables for females and all minorities. Included were recruitment, training, promotions, and incentive rewards.

Shortly thereafter, I left the FDA for a DC job in the General Services Administration as a policy analyst. I was assigned to the Contract Compliance Program, where I reviewed affirmative action plans nationwide. I served under Edward Mitchell, a World War II hero. He had the unique position of being a permanent GS-17.

Under reorganization three years later, we were merged with a Labor Department program called the Office of Federal Contract Compliance Program (OFCCP). I was offered a choice of a downgrade or transfer to Richmond, Virginia.

After lengthy discussion with my wife, Doris, we decided to move to Richmond, Virginia.

The government paid our moving expenses.

Chesterfield County was the second highest county in Virginia for excellence in education. We settled into a house in the Brandermill Community in Chesterfield County and remained there for the next twenty-seven years. Doris easily found a job with Johnston Willis Hospital, then located in Richmond, Virginia. Brandermill was fifteen miles from the city limits of Richmond, Virginia.

Along with my job with OFCCP, I was hired by Chesterfield County to teach tennis. Over several years, I was told I had the highest retention rate among all instructors. After three years with OFCCP, I was promoted to the GS-13 level at the Equal Employment Opportunity Commission (EEOC). My father, Wilbur Jenkins Sr., passed a few days before I reported. He had been ill for years with lung cancer. He and his wife, Edna, along with my half-sister Joan, lived in Newport News, Virginia.

While at EEOC, I was assigned to the supervisor of intake and fact finding. We worked hard, volunteering to carry cases home and work on Sundays. A sign-in sheet was necessary to get into the office!

We were commended by the district director, Cissy Meade, for excellent performance. Notably, I was able to secure senior workers from the Urban League and younger workers from CETA. Mr. Robert Dickover came to us from Baltimore, Maryland, to discuss a GS-14 promotion.

After leaving EEOC, I worked for a Virginia program dealing with affirmative action. Shortly thereafter, I was called to Ft. Lee for $12,000 more. I became the EEO specialist at the Troops Support Agency (TSA) run by Mr. James Canady.

I reviewed incoming data monthly for recruitment, training, promotions, and incentive awards for females and minorities. Later, we were merged into the Defense Commissary Agency (DCA). I traveled to the Pentagon and was able to get Pentagon officials to come to Fort Lee. I was publicly commended by my general for a Black history program. He had two stars and said it was the best program he had ever seen.

To my great distress, I lost a dear friend: Arthur Ashe!

The world I knew, including Bryant Gumbel, was devastated on air. Arthur Ashe had come onto the world stage as a poor person who was not allowed to play on the courts of Richmond, Virginia. Later on, he was given the *key* to the city and now has a street named after him and a statue in his honor.

For those who did not know, Nelson Mandela, after twenty-seven years in prison, was asked who the *first* person he wanted to see was. His answer was "Arthur Ashe."

That fact is a story in itself.

I met Arthur Ashe at an early age, about ten. He was skinny and self-effacing. For some reason, he liked me, and as he grew older, he asked my advice about a number of things. I was happy to oblige. At about seventeen years of age, Arthur was adopted by Pancho Ganozales. Pancho invited Arthur to a great tennis boot camp. He was drilled relentlessly on all types of shots, tactics, and strategies. No show of irritation was allowed. He had to eat, sleep, and dream tennis. Arthur told me, "I could not win a game, not even from Pancho Segura, Gonzales's running mate, who was from Ecuador and about 5'7 inches" tall.

As a minority male in a sport populated by Caucasians, Arthur Ashe had to exhibit good conduct along with good manners. Arthur was taught

Pancho's serve. If you ever go to Stade Roland Garros in Paris, France, you will see ten images of Pancho's serve.

At his peak, no one would touch him.

Arthur made the Junior Davis Cups team and later the Davis Cup Team, representing America all over the world. Why he left us so soon at age fifty, I will never understand. I was sad and depressed about Arthur's passing. I have a picture of Wilbur III, Kimberly, Arthur, and his wife at the wedding reception in 1977. Kimberly was seven, and Wilbur III was ten.

After I left DCA, I worked at several jobs. I taught tennis privately and at John Tyler's College, Chester branch. I also taught small business management and was rated by class members on a scale of one to seven with all sixes and sevens. I also taught inmates near Kings Dominion.

Ladies in My Life

The first lady I remember is my great-grandmother, known as Mother Julia. She was a midwife and attended my birth with Dr. Washington. I was blessed to be the apple of her eye.

The second lady I remember was Grandmother Jenny. She was based in Philadelphia, Pennsylvania.

The third lady was my mother, Gertrude Jenkins, later Mrs. Teasley. She thought the sun came up so that she could see me. She was married to my father for four and a half years.

The fourth lady in my life was the aforementioned Doris Ann Sroufe. She had shown a light in my life for forty-four years. She was an excellent registered nurse. She took care of our two kids and me for all of her life.

The fifth lady in my life was Vivian Malone, later Mrs. Jones. We dated briefly while single. She integrated the University of Alabama despite the state's racist governor, George Wallace. She received mail from all over the world! She was in Senator Robert Kennedy's party when the 1964 Civil Rights Bill was signed.

The sixth lady in my life is Kimberly Jeneece Jenkins, later Kimberly Robinson. She was my first scholar athlete at Clover Hill High. She was third in her class academically and lettered in two sports, track and tennis.

She graduated from the University of Virginia in Charlottesville, Virginia, with honors, and then Harvard Law School, from which she graduated cum laude.

As a mother, she birthed Sienna, now seven, and Naomi, now four.

She is married to Gerard T. Robinson, and they have a twenty-two-year-old daughter named Kamaria.

Men in My Life

First there is Dr. Thomas Calhoun, my best friend and a graduate of Florida A&M University and Meharry Medical School. He introduced me to my wife, Doris. He is a father of four and a retired Surgeon. We won National and local tennis tournaments.

The second man in my life was the aforementioned late, great Arthur Ashe.

The third man in my life is the late Wilbur Jenkins Sr. We were estranged for most of my life. His second wife was Edna, and his only daughter was Joan.

The fourth man in my life was the late Dr. Earl T. Cullins. He gave expert care to my mother for over eight years whenever she wanted to see him. He also brought her medicines to her house and never charged her a dime!

The fifth man in my life was the late Clarence Clyde Ferguson, Dean of Howard Law School. He used discretionary funds at the urging of Mrs. Jean Campher Cahn to help with legal expenses.

The sixth man in my life is Wilbur III, my only son. He plays the organ and piano and can paint well enough to sell on the street. He made a forty-five-minute movie. He graduated from Clover Hill High in Chesterfield County. He also lettered in tennis playing the number-one doubles and number-two singles at one point. He had a scholarship to Virginia Tech. He lasted there for two and a half years, finding himself in a class of four hundred people with a number.

Wilbur Jenkins III also went to J. Sargent Reynolds and VCU. He then moved to New York City, where he attended its School of Fine Arts. He works for a Law firm and does data entry and computer graphics.

The seventh man in my life is Melvin Curry. He was my neighbor who lived two doors down in Brandermill. He could start my car when I couldn't. Melvin was a West Virginian who worked with me at the Department of Labor. He and his wife, Francis, and two children, Angela and Leslie, were close family friends. Once when I had a Baltimore, Maryland, conference and Doris was in Ohio, my kids stayed with the Curry's. Melvin and I did a compliance review of Reynolds Metal. We discovered discrepancies in their affirmative action plan. They complained about us because they were not used to the questions we asked. Their complaint went nowhere because we acted within the guidelines.

Incidents in My Life

While stationed at my air force base in Germany, I received leave time. I went to Paris, France, and met Darlene Hard. She partnered with Althea Gibson in doubles was a finalist to her in singles, and defeated her partner in the mixed doubles at Wimbledon. We bonded and practiced together. She took me to a secret restaurant where players ate *free*! I was lucky to meet her.

As a student at St. Louis University, I met Carolyn Hester. At that time, she was the number-two singer in the country next to Joan Baez. I was number two in the American Tennis Association (ATA) next to Arthur Ashe. She saw me at the back of her coffeehouse, picked up a large bowl of ice cream, added a spoon for me, and introduced herself. Carolyn was gorgeous with hair down to her buttocks. She was later on the cover of *Collier's* magazine. We bonded as friends. Later in Washington DC, she introduced me to Godfrey Cambridge. I was invited to spend the night in separate quarters.

While competing in the ATA finals against New Yorker Billy Davis, I served an ace on match point. Mr. Maceo Hill captured the ace on camera. The official was about to call the match when a lineman who had been sleeping called, "Out!" On my second serve, Billy hit a net cord return on a ball he thought was out. I was disheartened and later lost the match in five sets.

Interesting Events in My Life

At the end of age seven, Wilbur III was hospitalized. My wife, Doris, an excellent nurse, suggested 60 percent of one medicine and 40 percent of the other to the two doctors treating him. He began to get better after her suggestion.

In addition, Wilbur III was getting nightly injections requiring three nurses—two to hold him and one to use the needle. I prayed about this situation, and an answer was given to me. This answer was nothing I had read or seen in a movie. I was just inspired to talk to my son in a prayerful voice and to have him grasp my hands as tightly as he could. While doing this, I told him he would no longer require three nurses; one would be enough. I told him that my strength was being transferred to him as a result of my prayer. He believed me and never required three nurses again. I thank God for this inspiration!

In Atlanta, Georgia, in 2007, my son was having problems getting work. I prayed that he would soon find an answer to the problem. In New York City, the unemployment rate for Black males was 50 percent.

Within seven days, *he got a position offered* to him that would allow him to hire people under him if he could not meet the workload. He had not held a similar position before or since.

While in Germany in the Air Force, assigned to Spangdahlem Air Force Base, I was chatting with another Black airman, and we were interrupted by a Caucasian airman. He stated that he had overheard my conversation about my playing on Tennis Team and that I was not good enough to make the team traveling back to the United States. I will call him Al.

I stepped back from Al, not being used to a stranger telling me what I could not do. I asked him, "Do you know my name?"

"No" was the answer.

"Do you know where I played?"

"No" was the answer.

I looked at him and said, "We'll see." He did not know that I had had a tennis scholarship to Florida A&M College, in Tallahassee, Florida. We had participated in the Tuskegee, Alabama, Southern Intercollegiate Athletic Conference (SIAC) Championships. I was the number-six player and the number-three doubles player. We swept singles and doubles, one to six singles and one to three doubles!

I was determined that I would prove Al wrong. I doubled my efforts on the track and on the hardball courts. I learned to play soft finesse and hard shots. With this effort, I won the doubles championship and was a finalist in the singles. Later, I reached the quarterfinals for the Command Championship and was named to the All United States Air Force in Europe (USAFE) Team to go to the States.

I was the only minority and only enlisted man on the team.

I called AL when I got back and offered him a copy of the *All-World Air Force Times* with a story about me and a picture. He refused my offer and stated he was going out for the Basketball squad team.

Al was sitting on the bench when we won the Basketball championship.

I was the high point man!

Tennis in Germany

While assigned as an airman in the early fifties, I decided to train my lungs and legs. I was aided by Hans Loft, a former German paratrooper. He was second to Jesse Owens in the 1936 Olympics. He showed me a clipping. He trained the airmen on the base.

I was later adopted by Captain White, a Doctor who introduced me to a Major at the base. We became partners and won the doubles championships for the Twelfth Air Force. He was a Californian and played mixed doubles with Louise Brough, a Wimbledon doubles champion. She also lost to Althea Gibson in the Forest Hills Finals in 1957, the first time a Negro had won a major tennis tournament

I later met Rene Ruguis, a Yugoslavian who played tennis doubles when the Yugoslavians had the best team in Europe. Rene spoke French, German, English, Russian, and a native dialect. Rene and I went to a local nightclub and met two "B" girls, one German and one French. Rene kept up a trilingual conversation with no problems.

We took the dance floor and were noticed by the crowd. When we decided to leave, the "B" girls said no and bought us drinks.

"B" girls got non-alcoholic drinks and were paid to converse and dance with customers.

Later, Rene introduced me to his fiancée. She was wealthy and lived two blocks away from the palace in Monaco. Grace Kelly, the movie star, and the prince lived at the palace. Rene and his fiancée granted me a standing invitation to visit and stay as long as I wanted! On one occasion, Rene and I won the doubles match in a weekend tournament. We later lost in the semifinals.

I later met Hans, the former German paratrooper at Spangdahlem Air Force Base in Germany in 1954. He gave me the airmen's physical fitness drills. He liked me after noticing that he never heard me curse or be rude to anyone. I was then running five miles a day, Monday through Friday. I rested on Saturday and Sunday. He asked his young son to call me Uncle Jenkins. Later, he pulled a picture from his wallet, showing him finishing second to the great Jesse Owens in the 1936 Olympics in the two hundred meters.

Blair Underwood

While working at Fort Lee in Richmond, in the 1980s, I was invited to an army presentation. There, I met the parents of Hollywood actor Blair Underwood. Later, when his mother found out that I was a tennis instructor, she asked for lessons for her and her youngest daughter, which I provided for several months.

NOTE FROM KIMBERLY JENKINS ROBINSON

I am the only daughter of Wilbur Hampton Jenkins Jr. and his youngest child. It has been such a pleasure to read about some of the life experiences of my father and his lifelong friend Dr. Calhoun in this book. I add this note to share a few of my favorite memories of him.

My dad was not only my father; he also was my tennis coach and greatest fan as well as a civil rights advocate. As a dad and a coach, he always pushed me to be my best. He used to pay us for A grades that we brought home on our report cards. When I once brought home all As and an A-, he asked me if I could bring up the A-. Apparently, my response was "Daaaaaad," with great frustration, but I still brought up the A- to an A.

My dad was a demanding tennis coach. We spent many hours on the tennis court together, and he taught me not just about tennis but also about the volleys of life during those sessions. One of my favorite memories is when he said, "There are three types of people in this life. There are turkeys, pigeons, and eagles. Turkeys never get their bottoms off of the ground. Pigeons can fly but never soar. Eagles, however, can soar among the clouds. And there are no turkeys in this family."

So, I strove to be an eagle all of my childhood, and his words still challenge me to excellence today.

I believe that tennis helped my dad live the long and full life that he lived. He played until six months before he had a stroke in 2017, and he was eighty-three years old at that time. He was very active and enjoyed playing with friends, including his dear friend and student Marco Harris, who became like a second son to Dad. I think that tennis helped Dad stay young in mind, body, and spirit.

I recall that when we moved to Midlothian, Virginia, in 1979, my parents shared that we moved so that my brother and I could attend better public schools. Both of my parents emphasized that it was essential that I get the best education that I could. They shared stories of attending segregated schools and made sure that I knew how fortunate I was to attend integrated, high-quality public schools. When we moved to Midlothian in 1979, the schools were definitely more challenging than the ones I had originally attended. I remain grateful for the strong foundation that they created for my life and work.

I decided to become a lawyer in many ways to model my dad's life work. He not only was active in the civil rights movement, but Wilbur Jenkins Jr. also dedicated his career as a lawyer to fighting discrimination. We heard many stories of discrimination that he was addressing at work around the dinner table. This helped me to understand that discrimination endured but that lawyers could make a difference in remedying it. This led me to want to make a difference in the lives of others and help those who had suffered injustice. I decided to become a lawyer in high school.

I recall that when I was in Harvard Law School, one of my professors did not call on Black students in the class of 140 students. Some of the other Black students in the Black Law Schools Association wanted to stage a protest, as did I. I shared this with my dad and asked his thoughts. He told me, "Choose your battles wisely." He said that I was at Harvard Law School to get the best legal education that I could and that I should not let anything distract me from that. He said that this professor would be there long after I had left, but I only had one shot at learning all that I could at Harvard Law School. The advice to choose my battles wisely is advice that I have recalled on numerous occasions, and it has served me well.

I am currently an endowed professor at the University of Virginia School of Law, one of the top law schools in the country. I teach and write about civil rights and the importance of equal educational opportunity. My dad's lifelong dedication to civil rights greatly influenced my career path. I have sometimes wondered where I would be if my parents had not made the decision to move our family so that my brother and I could attend better public schools. In my work on education, I have a deep sense of gratitude to God and my parents for allowing me to experience an excellent education.

My father was a man of faith, and he embraced his Catholic upbringing. My mother, Doris Sroufe Jenkins, had to convert to Catholicism for the Catholic Church to marry them. My parents raised our family in the Catholic Church, and I attribute my faith in Jesus Christ in part to that foundation. My dad once shared with me how he was riding his bike along a busy road, and he felt something lift him off the road and drop him into the bushes. Then a car went by exactly where he would have been riding. He believed an angel saved his life. I believe this too and that angels intercede in our lives without us knowing it.

I am blessed that my dad was a loving father-in-law to my husband, Gerard, and grandfather to our daughters, Sienna Robinson, now thirteen; Naomi Robinson, now ten; and Kamaria Robinson, now twenty-eight. My dad enjoyed talking about current events with Gerard, and he always thought very highly of him. My dad also taught Sienna to play tennis beginning at the age of five. She still remembers his guidance, such as hit the ball low to high. He adored his granddaughters.

In the days right after my dad passed, I read a story about a father who had told his daughter when she was experiencing a difficult season in her life that "Every storm in your life is followed by a rainbow."[16] Later that afternoon, I saw a rainbow. For me, this felt like a clear sign from the Lord that my father was with Him and that brighter days lay ahead.

---

[16] Gail Gabrielle, "Comfort from Beyond," in *Believe in Miracles: 101 Stories of Hope, Answered Prayers, and Divine Intervention*, ed. Amy Newark (2020), 262.

Thank you, Dad, for all that you taught me
and for your steadfast love for me.
—Kimberly Jenkins Robinson

ABOUT THE AUTHORS

The authors, Dr. Thomas Calhoun and Wilbur H. Jenkins Jr.(Jenk), JD, are shown with their wives Shirley Jones and Doris Sroufe.

Calhoun and Jenkins, along with seven members of the Black Hawks, grew up within four blocks of each other in Jacksonville, Florida.

They both went to St. Pius Catholic School, where they were taught by the strict Sisters of Saint Joseph and Jesuit priests. Calhoun was a grade ahead of Jenk and was baptized a Catholic.

After graduating from Stanton High School, they both went to Florida Agricultural and Mechanical College (FAMC) in Tallahassee, Florida, in 1950, where they became members of the tennis team.

Jenk left FAMC after the first semester and joined the US Air Force, where he spent four years.

In 1953, FAMC became a university, FAMU.

Calhoun went on to become Captain of the tennis team and won the National Intercollegiate Singles Championships for Historically Black Colleges in 1952.

He graduated in 1954 with a Bachelor of Science in pre-medicine and became a Second Lieutenant from the Reserve Officers' Training Corps (ROTC) of the US Army.

He and Jenk would reunite in 1955 after Jenk was honorable discharged from the Air Force and in 1956 and 1957, during which time they played tennis on the American Tennis Association (ATA) circuit.

Calhoun went to graduate school and taught Biology at Fisk University in Nashville, Tennessee, prior to their playing tennis in 1957.

Calhoun received a Doctor of Medicine degree (MD) from Meharry Medical College in Nashville, Tennessee, in 1963 and completed a residency in General Surgery from Howard University in 1968.

He taught at the medical school at Howard University and practiced surgery in the Washington DC Metropolitan area for thirty years.

Following the anthrax event in DC in 2001, when two postal workers died from anthrax poisoning, he obtained a Master of Science (MS) degree in Biohazardous Threat Agents and Emerging Infectious Diseases from Georgetown University in DC in 2007.

A memorable event during grad school was a visit to the Central Intelligence Agency in Langley, Virginia. (See picture, Author in the burgundy shirt.)

He retired from the practice of surgery in 2003 and is an Emeritus Clinical Associate Professor of Surgery at Howard University.

He lives in Washington DC with his wife, Shirley, and children, Thomas Junior, Christine, and Kathy.

Their youngest daughter, Maria, was killed in an automobile accident in August of 2003.

After the 1957 ATA circuit, Jenk enrolled at Saint Louis University, and after graduation with a Bachelor of Science (BS) in Psychology, he entered law school at Howard University, in Washington, DC, from which he received a Juris Doctorate in 1968.

He married Doris Sroufe, a registered nurse, and they had two children and three grandchildren.

Jenk and Calhoun played in their last tennis tournament in the finals of the 80s Doubles, at the 100th Anniversary of the ATA on August 2, 2017, in Baltimore, Maryland, the site of where the first ATA tournament was played in 1917, losing to Walter Moore and Leon Bowser 5–7 and 0–6.

Jenk relates his memories under "I, Wilbur Hampton Jenkins Jr."

Dr. Thomas Calhoun and Shirley Calhoun

Wilbur H. Jenkins Jr., Juris Doctorate
Doris Jenkin59

Printed in the United States
by Baker & Taylor Publisher Services